DRIVING LOYALTY

DRIVING LOYALTY

TURNING EVERY CUSTOMER AND EMPLOYEE INTO A RAVING FAN FOR YOUR BRAND

KIRK KAZANJIAN

CROWN BUSINESS
NEW YORK

Published in the United States by Crown Business, an imprint of the Crown Publishing Group, a division of Random House, Inc., New York.
www.crownpublishing.com

CROWN BUSINESS is a trademark and CROWN and the Rising Sun colophon are registered trademarks of Random House, Inc.

Crown Business books are available at special discounts for bulk purchases for sales promotions or corporate use. Special editions, including personalized covers, excerpts of existing books, or books with corporate logos, can be created in large quantities for special needs. For more information, contact Premium Sales at (212) 572-2232 or e-mail specialmarkets@randomhouse.com.

Library of Congress Cataloging-in-Publication Data
Kazanjian, Kirk.
Driving loyalty / Kirk Kazanjian.—1st ed.
p. cm.
Includes index.
1. Customer service. 2. Loyalty. 3. Corporate culture.
4. Organizational behavior. 5. Brand loyalty. 6. Customer loyalty.
I. Title.
HF5415.5.K387 2007
658.8'343—dc23 2012033231

ISBN 978-0-385-34694-8
eISBN 978-0-385-34695-5

Printed in the United States of America

Book design by Lauren Dong
Jacket design by Michael Nagin

10 9 8 7 6 5 4 3 2 1

First Edition

Contents

Foreword

When my father, Jack, started his business in 1957, he didn't have a lot to build on. Not far removed from a stint in the navy, he found himself in a lower-level office in a St. Louis Cadillac dealership with a fleet of seven cars and just one other employee. That, plus his reputation and entrepreneurial drive, was all he had to work with. But he and others shaped by their experiences in World War II believed very strongly in the simple idea of doing the right thing. The ideals of integrity, hard work, and team spirit inevitably helped his referral-based business to grow and flourish.

Today Enterprise Holdings and its operating subsidiaries constitute the largest car rental company in the world. We built the Enterprise Rent-A-Car brand and now own the Alamo Rent A Car and National Car Rental brands as well. We have more than seventy thousand employees, operate in forty countries, posted annual revenues of nearly $15 billion in 2012, and have become one of the largest privately held family businesses in North America.

Those numbers seem pretty staggering when you consider that my father never started out with grand ambitions. He simply wanted to build an honest business known for taking good care of its customers and employees. He believed that if you operated with that philosophy, and developed a strong reputation as a result, profitability and intense loyalty were bound to follow.

It sounds very simple, and it is. But few companies are truly committed to these principles. Those that are often fail in the execution. We've spent a lot of time perfecting what we like to refer to around here as our "secret sauce," and we're gratified by the results. Enterprise brands consistently rank at the top of customer service surveys, our employee retention rates are among the highest of any industry, and we are regularly recognized in various national rankings as a great place to work.

Because of this, we are constantly being asked by other companies to share the Enterprise formula for driving customer and employee loyalty. Few people understand our secret sauce better than Kirk Kazanjian. Kirk and I first met nearly a decade ago. He has since spent considerable time studying our organization to uncover those principles we have developed over the years to drive loyalty in our customers and employees. He believes, as do I, that these principles can help any business to become stronger and more successful.

Kirk first touched on our customer service techniques in his best-selling book *Exceeding Customer Expectations*. Five years later, *Driving Loyalty* takes the story to the next level and provides tangible advice that you can begin to use right away.

A lot has changed since Kirk's first book was published. Our founding values and general approach are the same, but we've learned a lot and expanded our thinking in ways that have been very beneficial. For instance, we previously believed that organic growth was the best way to build our business, and long avoided even the temptation of undertaking an acquisition of any significant size. We had a great business model and didn't want to weaken the culture we had worked so hard to build. But when the opportunity to purchase Alamo and National came up in 2007, we realized that we had to be more open-minded. My family ultimately decided to buy these brands after realizing they would help to strengthen our business, increase our airport presence, and lead to even greater loyalty among our customers and employees. Frankly, this transaction has worked out better than I could have expected, and we have now become the biggest player both in the home-city market and at airports.

I want to emphasize that we are not perfect. Far from it. But we truly believe in putting customers and employees first in everything we do, knowing that loyalty will follow. As Kirk points out, we do this in numerous ways. We've come up with some unique methods for engaging our workforce by treating them as owners and providing meaningful financial and professional rewards in return for their commitment to the business. We also give them powerful incentives to wow every customer who walks in our door, which has led to the highest satisfaction scores in the industry.

In addition, we increasingly look for new ways to enhance the customer experience. We do this by continually training our workforce, using the techniques you'll read about in this book. We delight customers through technology, too. If you're not doing the same, you'll be left behind in today's wired world, where increasingly the best service involves conducting the entire transaction electronically.

Teamwork also plays a huge role at our company, in terms of both our employees and the numerous corporate partnerships we have developed over the years. Many of our loyal partners have been by our side for decades, allowing us to develop an array of mutually rewarding relationships that have taken our business to a level that would not have been possible otherwise. More recently, we continue to deploy considerable resources—financial and otherwise—toward becoming a more sustainable company, initiating some of the most comprehensive plans I am aware of for reducing emissions and otherwise helping the environment. As you'll read in this book, not only is that good for our planet, but it's yet another important driver of customer and employee loyalty.

I trust you will find many ways to incorporate some of the secret sauce we have cooked up over the years into your own business. In fact, many of these principles can be applied to your personal career as well, allowing you to stand head and shoulders above the competition. They certainly have worked well for us over the course of nearly sixty years, and I can promise you they will remain the compass by which we conduct ourselves over the many decades to come.

Andrew C. Taylor, Chairman and CEO,
Enterprise Holdings, Inc.

Introduction

In order to build a successful business in today's hypercompetitive world, it's essential to have an army of loyal customers and employees. Few companies understand this better than Enterprise Holdings, which has quietly grown from the basement of a Midwest auto dealership into the world's largest car rental company.

Enterprise has achieved much of its success by following a simple philosophy espoused by founder Jack Taylor back at the company's founding: "Take care of your customers and employees first, and the profits will follow." By putting customer and employee loyalty at the heart of everything it does, Enterprise has transformed itself into one of the biggest privately held, family-owned businesses ever created. It has built a unique model for wowing customers and maintaining an engaged and dedicated workforce. It has also discovered how to use the power of technology, full-spectrum marketing, and select partnerships to help expand its mission and fuel the bottom line.

In *Driving Loyalty*, you'll get an inside look at Enterprise's secrets for outsmarting the competition by treating both customers and employees like royalty. It's a proven formula that brings customers back again and again, while attracting employees who stay with the company for the long term.

The principles Enterprise lives by provide an excellent case study for how any business can offer exceptional customer service, create a high-performing work environment, and build an enormously successful company. In addition to winning numerous awards for customer service excellence, Enterprise has long been known for being one of the best companies to work for. Its unique structure allows employees to make autonomous decisions, free of needless bureaucracy. It also ties compensation directly to customer service survey results and company profits.

Enterprise has operated under the radar for much of its history (which was part of the company's overall business strategy). Several years ago, the company opened its doors to me for the first time to share the Enterprise Rent-A-Car customer service story. The resulting book, *Exceeding Customer Expectations*, was named one of the 30 Best Business Books of 2007 by Soundview Executive Book Summaries.

While the basics remain, much has changed since *Exceeding Customer Expectations* was written. For one thing, Enterprise was a stand-alone business back then. The company has subsequently restructured and now owns Alamo Rent A Car and National Car Rental as well, thanks to an enormously successful acquisition that was almost immediately accretive to earnings, despite predictions to the contrary from some industry insiders. Enterprise also went counter to its own original thinking, since initially the company frowned on the idea of purchasing large competitors, preferring to grow organically instead.

Indeed, Enterprise has tweaked and refined a number of its business practices in recent years, allowing the company to report a continuous stream of revenue increases, even in a challenging economy. What's more, by implementing the principles revealed in this book, the customer service and employee retention scores for Enterprise, Alamo, and National have all significantly improved.

In *Driving Loyalty*, you'll discover the lessons that have turned Enterprise into the fifteenth-largest private company in the world. You'll learn how to think differently, engage your workforce more effectively, lead with empathy, deliver dazzling customer service, market effectively online and off, and let customers fuel your company's growth in order to generate a powerful bottom line.

At its heart, *Driving Loyalty* is a guide to running an employee-centered company that caters to its customers. You'll learn how applying these proven, timeless values to virtually any business can lead to exceptional performance.

Each chapter in this book is devoted to a different element of building loyalty with your customers and employees. Enterprise does this in tangible ways, such as picking customers up and bringing them to the branch to retrieve their rental car. But it also does this through carefully planned messaging, including marketing campaigns that emphasize engagement and using targeted media with specific audiences in mind. What's more, every technology project starts out by first answering the question "How will this enhancement improve the overall experience for customers and employees?"

Driving Loyalty also highlights lessons from other companies that have successfully employed similar techniques, to offer a full array of ideas that can be put to work in your own business.

In the pages that follow, you will learn:

- Why taking care of your customers and employees builds loyalty and increases profitability
- How being different from the competition can give you a big edge
- Ways to identify the kinds of employees who will remain loyal for decades
- Why paying workers well can actually put more money into your company's coffers
- Strategies for offering exceptional customer service that lead to significant increased business
- The principles for building high-performing teams
- Why simply keeping customers *satisfied* isn't enough (you need to exceed their expectations)
- How to track company and employee performance in a meaningful way

- Why forming strong partnerships can take your company to the next level
- The best ways to grow your business and expand your target markets without sacrificing the customer experience
- The keys to integrating different cultures into your organization
- How to adapt your message based on shifting market and industry trends
- Ways to build brand loyalty, and why the rules differ based on your target audience
- Which techniques work best when it comes to surveying customers and employees
- The formula for effectively leveraging social media, while integrating it into your other marketing efforts as a way to connect with your customers and employees
- Why members of your IT team, especially in smaller companies, should start by working in the trenches
- Proven strategies for attracting desirable workers in a competitive hiring environment
- Why focusing on sustainability is about more than just being a good corporate citizen (it can make you a lot of money, too)
- How to protect your most valuable asset—your brand
- Why you should share your company's financial successes with your employees in order to get to the next level
- Techniques for making first-rate customer service a way of life for every member of your team

In the coming chapters, you'll discover how to put some of the Enterprise magic to work in your own company, thus helping to drive incredible loyalty and positioning your business to grow beyond your wildest dreams.

We'll start by taking a closer look at Enterprise's history, including the previously untold story of how it came to acquire National and Alamo several years ago. We'll also talk about the process the company went through in deciding whether to keep all three brands, and how doing so allowed it to reach a much larger audience of loyal customers. We'll then explore what Enterprise does to engage its workforce, including the management techniques it uses to drive productivity and retention. Next we'll talk about Enterprise's proven approach for exceeding customer expectations, both through its employees and increasingly through the effective use of technology as well. The last few chapters are devoted to several other important elements of driving loyalty among your customers and employees, such as the most effective marketing strategies in today's very noisy world, the best ways to grow and expand your business, the importance of forming key partnerships, and why it's critical to operate in a sustainable manner.

By uncovering the secrets that Enterprise and other well-respected companies use to instill loyalty, you'll be armed with the key tenets needed to find and retain fantastic employees, build a global brand, provide excellent service, and achieve tremendous success regardless of what industry you're in or what type of customer you are trying to reach.

1 Think Differently

The world's greatest visionaries and entrepreneurs share several important traits. They are natural born leaders with big dreams and a bit of a rebellious edge. They are willing to take risks, without fear of failure. They are passionate about what they do. And, perhaps most of all, they think differently, approaching problems that others have failed to tackle in new or better ways.

Among the modern-day business executives at the top of this list are people such as Steve Jobs, Walt Disney, Bill Gates, Warren Buffett, Mark Zuckerberg, Charles Schwab, Jeff Bezos, Sam Walton, and Phil Knight. The list also includes a number of famous corporate pairings, such as Larry Page and Sergey Brin, Ben Cohen and Jerry Greenfield, and Jack and Andy Taylor.

If you've never heard of Jack Taylor or his son, Andy, before, you're certainly familiar with at least some of their businesses. Jack is the founder of Enterprise Holdings, parent company of Enterprise Rent-A-Car, Alamo Rent A Car, and National Car Rental. Andy has run the company and overseen its incredible growth for more than two decades. The Taylor family also owns a portfolio of other companies, all of which are built around a very simple philosophy: "Take care of your customers and employees first, and the profits will follow." While most businesses pay lip service to the importance of customer service, the entire Enterprise organization is structured around this goal.

Since 1957, Enterprise has operated under the premise that employees should be treated as owners—and paid as such—while being held fully accountable for consistently exceeding customer expectations. Every corporate decision and new initiative is enacted based on how it will improve the overall customer experience and make life easier for employees. This strategy has resulted in extremely high levels of customer and employee loyalty, along with an ongoing, profitable revenue stream. In fact, Jack's initial investment of $10,000 has blossomed into a company that is now worth billions of dollars.

TAKE CARE OF THE CUSTOMER

Jack Taylor's notion of how to operate a business was largely influenced by his midwestern upbringing. A member of the "Greatest Generation," Jack never liked school and admittedly wasn't the best student. He ultimately dropped out of college after less than two years to join the military following the attack on Pearl Harbor. Jack became an officer in World War II, serving as a navy pilot flying combat missions in a Grumman F6F Hellcat off the decks of the USS *Essex* and the USS *Enterprise* in the Pacific Theater.

Being in the military drove home the importance of teamwork. "The beauty of teamwork is its simplicity," Jack observes. "Everybody is in the right place, the leader points the way, and you all move together as one." This notion played a big role in how he shaped his company.

A lifelong entrepreneur, Jack started what ultimately became Enterprise Rent-A-Car on the lower level of a St. Louis Cadillac dealership, originally as a leasing business. Back then, few companies offered car leases, and Jack saw this as an opportunity with significant growth potential. Jack had previously enjoyed great success as a car salesman and knew the industry well. In his mind, leasing was an even better business than having your own car dealership, since at the time individuals could secure the rights to only one franchise location from a given manufacturer. With leasing, the opportunity for expansion was unlimited.

For the first couple of years, Jack had just one employee, his administrative assistant. But because of his commitment to taking care of customers, the business began to grow. The company, which was known as Enterprise Leasing back then, lost $30,000 its first year, broke even the second, and recorded a profit of $60,000 in year three. “It took ten years before we made our first million,” Jack recalls. “But aside from year one, we have been a profitable entity ever since.”

PUT A NEW SPIN ON A FAMILIAR INDUSTRY

By the early 1960s, the car rental industry was dominated by a few national brands, with offices located almost exclusively at the airports. It was virtually impossible for an upstart to get into the business, as the cost of going head-to-head with established players such as Hertz and Avis was too high. For that reason, Jack had no interest in competing in the traditional car rental industry, given that it was so cutthroat and crowded. Instead, he noticed that his leasing customers were increasingly interested in getting cars for just a day or two, to serve as loaners for out-of-town guests or replacements when their own vehicles were being serviced. Jack and his small team sensed opportunity and launched a rental car division in 1963.

Enterprise Rent-A-Car took a much different approach. Instead of operating at airports, Enterprise built a reputation as the home-city car rental company. It was the place you could turn to when your vehicle was in the shop, or when you didn’t want to put miles on your own automobile for a short weekend trip. Given the demand in this untapped market, Enterprise quietly earned a leadership position in the neighborhood rental car segment. The company continued to grow in cities around the country largely under the radar of other competitors. Years later it began to establish a presence at some airports as well.

Jack recognized early on that when you have a commodity business, with many competitors offering essentially the same thing, unless you do something unique to differentiate yourself, customers will base their decision on whom to go with primarily on price, showing no loyalty to any particular brand. But if you are able to put a fresh twist on the otherwise ordinary, people are more likely to choose your product or service without even looking at the competition, because they know it will make for a better overall experience. This explains why companies such as Enterprise, FedEx, Starbucks, Costco, JetBlue, Amazon.com, and Chobani have all been so successful.

FedEx founder Fred Smith saw inefficiencies in the air-freight industry that caused shipments to take far longer to get delivered than he thought was necessary. This prompted Smith to research how to build a more efficient distribution system, work he started in a term paper as a Yale undergraduate in 1965. Armed with fourteen small aircraft at the Memphis airport, Smith began operating what was originally known as Federal Express on April 13, 1973. The company went up against traditional freight carriers, United Parcel Service, and the seemingly venerable United States Postal Service. Federal Express stood out by offering much faster service for those shipments that, as the company's ads used to say, absolutely, positively had to be there overnight. Such speedy service came at a higher cost, but to business customers, this premium was worth it. Plus, the notion of having the ability to track a package's progress and know for certain when a delivery would arrive won significant customer loyalty, allowing FedEx to become the first American start-up to reach $1 billion in revenues through organic growth.

Starbucks opened its first location in Seattle's Pike Place Market in 1971, but it wasn't until Howard Schultz joined the company more than a decade later that executives began to think about how to make this true commodity business stand out. While on a business trip to Milan, Schultz was impressed by the popularity of Italy's espresso bars and saw the potential to bring many of these same characteristics to the United States. He realized the right mix of beverages could create a sense of community, making a trip to Starbucks an *experience* rather than just a way to get a quick cup of java—something you could do at almost any restaurant. This mind-set earned Starbucks tremendous loyalty and allowed it to charge premium prices for otherwise ordinary beverages, fueling growth that now includes some seventeen thousand stores in forty-eight countries.

Sol Price changed the retail industry in 1976 by pioneering the discount membership warehouse club concept. Although retail stores were a dime a dozen, Price tweaked the business model to offer a relatively small selection of items that were sold in bulk at lower per-unit prices. He made the economics work by cutting overhead, offering no-frills service, and forcing customers to pay an annual fee for the privilege of shopping in the stores. The concept was an immediate hit. People loved the idea of getting bigger quantities for less, and their intense loyalty to the store was heightened by the fact that they had prepaid the cost of admission and felt they had better get their money's worth by frequenting it often. By 1992, there were ninety-four Price Clubs in the United States, Canada, and Mexico. Price Club merged with Costco in 1993, taking on the latter's name and creating an industry leader that continues to thrive.

Amazon.com founder Jeff Bezos saw the potential of tapping into the power of the Internet to bring efficiencies of scale to the largely commoditized business of selling books. While the largest brick-and-mortar bookstore was capable of carrying only around two hundred thousand titles, online you could stock every book imaginable. What's more, because the cost of operating in a virtual environment was significantly lower, Amazon was able to sell these books for much less than traditional retailers. The company also found a way to fulfill and deliver these orders fast. Amazon was a hit from its July 1995 launch, garnering significant publicity and loyal customers who enjoyed the added convenience and cheaper pricing for books, as well as

CDs, videos, and related items. Amazon has continued to transform the retail industry, branching out into everything from electronics to footwear, forever changing the way people shop.

When JetBlue's first flight pushed back from Terminal 6 at New York's JFK Airport on February 11, 2000, bound for Fort Lauderdale, it was the culmination of a dream for founder David Neeleman. Like Jack and Andy Taylor, Neeleman is an entrepreneur who had been involved in numerous start-ups over the years, mostly in the travel industry. Neeleman learned a lot about the airline business during a short stint at Southwest Airlines. He knew that the only way for a new carrier to survive was by offering something very different in the marketplace. His answer was to create an airline that, as he put it, was dedicated to bringing "humanity" back to air travel. By taking good care of customers and crew members, the airline built a reputation for having great service, happy employees, and extremely loyal customers. On top of that, the in-flight experience was unlike any other, with TV screens behind each passenger seat, free snacks, and clean new planes. This approach helped JetBlue become the most successful airline start-up in a generation, and though Neeleman has since left to start yet another airline, JetBlue continues to thrive.

More recently, Hamdi Ulukaya built a $1 billion success by thinking differently in the fast-growing and supercompetitive yogurt industry. Back in 2004, Kraft Foods decided to get out of the yogurt business, leaving a plant in upstate New York idle. Ulukaya, who grew up in Turkey, had a wholesale feta-cheese-making business in Johnstown, New York, having learned the craft from his father. While sorting through his mail one night in 2005, Ulukaya spotted a postcard from a real estate agent advertising the vacant Kraft yogurt plant. He initially threw the card away with the rest of his junk mail, but later he started to think about the possibilities. He could buy the facility and use it to make Greek yogurt, a very common treat in his native Turkey but then barely a blip in the U.S. yogurt category. Ulukaya purchased the plant for $700,000 and began to make his vision a reality with the launch of Chobani Greek yogurt in 2007. Ulukaya says his success formula is pretty simple. He uses only natural ingredients, has built a strong online following, and has tapped into the overall trend toward healthy eating. Because the whey is strained off when making Greek yogurt, it is creamier, higher in protein, and lower in fat. But since it takes more milk to manufacture, it is much more expensive than regular yogurt. That higher price hasn't dissuaded consumers. Chobani now commands 57 percent of the U.S. Greek yogurt market and 19 percent of the total U.S. yogurt category. Chobani's loyal customers wouldn't even consider eating another brand. What's ironic is that Kraft subsequently got back into the Greek yogurt business after witnessing Chobani's success, only to end its Athenos line in 2012 after failing to gain traction.

Ten Ways to Stand Out from the Competition and Drive Customer Loyalty

1. Meet an overlooked customer need.
2. Serve a specific and uncrowded niche.
3. Be willing to take risks.
4. Position yourself as an expert in your industry.
5. Dedicate yourself to delivering excellent service.
6. Find ways to reinvent existing operating models.
7. Offer something your competitors don't.
8. Be humble and authentic, in order to truly connect with your customers and employees.
9. Always be on the lookout for potential opportunities.
10. Never rest on your laurels.

HAVE A UNIQUE PROPOSITION

Like the other companies mentioned above, Enterprise has long been doing business very differently than everyone else. Among its innovations was becoming the first rental car company to pick up customers and bring them to their waiting vehicle.

Enterprise has also expanded into several other auto-related businesses over the years, including fleet services (the old leasing division), retail used car sales, truck rentals, and hourly car sharing. The company even thinks differently about how it buys and manages its rental fleet. Rather than leasing cars from automakers, Enterprise has long purchased its cars outright, a practice now being mimicked by many of its competitors. This allows the company to gain a cost advantage that pays dividends all the way through to when the vehicle is ultimately put out on the resale market.

Jack, who today at age ninety looks a lot like a silver-haired Cary Grant, turned over day-to-day management to his son, Andy, back in 1990. Andy inherited many of Jack's traits and has continued the tradition of building the company to be different from the competition while earning incredible customer and employee loyalty. Like Jack, Andy believes in seizing opportunity when it strikes, and with Jack's support, Enterprise acquired Vanguard Holdings, parent company of Alamo Rent A Car and National Car Rental, when it went on the market in 2007. Since then, the company has instilled the lessons about driving loyalty that you are about to learn across all three brands, sending customer service scores significantly higher in just a few short years. In a moment we'll explore how the company has been able to do this. But first let's take a look at how one of the most successful acquisitions in corporate history came to be, and see why expanding your business to serve different target markets is a powerful way to drive loyalty.

KEYS TO DRIVING LOYALTY BY THINKING DIFFERENTLY

1. Take care of your customers and employees first; the profits will follow.
2. Base every corporate initiative on how it will improve the overall customer experience and make life easier for employees.
3. Look to solve problems that others haven't tackled or find new ways to accomplish otherwise routine activities.
4. Create a cohesive environment and a strong sense of teamwork that foster customer satisfaction and higher employee retention.
5. Look to do business in locations and markets where your competitors aren't.
6. Differentiate your offerings—even if that means putting a twist on the otherwise ordinary—so that customers don't choose to do business with you based solely on price.
7. Be ready to seize opportunity when it strikes.

2 Be Open to Opportunity

While Enterprise's decision to buy Vanguard Holdings seems obvious in retrospect, it almost didn't happen. You see, for the first five decades of the company's history, Enterprise was focused exclusively on growing organically. While it had bought a few small rental car companies here and there, these were generally mom-and-pop operators with locations in different home-city markets. Enterprise had no ambitions of getting big fast through buying a large competitor.

Nevertheless, sometimes you have to be willing to look for ways to grow outside of your comfort zone, particularly when you are offered what seems to be the perfect fat pitch. You just don't want to undertake anything of this nature without careful evaluation to make sure it's the right fit from multiple perspectives—always keeping your customers and employees in mind.

BROADEN YOUR CUSTOMER BASE THROUGH ACQUISITION

Enterprise chairman and CEO Andy Taylor had been approached about buying Vanguard, which owned Alamo and National, several times in the past. Vanguard seemed to be on the market regularly, having gone through numerous owners over its history. It even traded publicly for a time before being acquired out of bankruptcy by the private equity firm Cerberus Capital Management in 2003.

Each time Enterprise had been asked to buy Vanguard before, it passed. The company just wasn't interested in taking on an acquisition of this size. Its organic growth strategy was working just fine, and purchasing another big company might put its customer- and employee-focused culture in jeopardy—something Andy and Jack Taylor weren't about to risk.

Enterprise didn't need to acquire another business to continue its impressive growth. It had become the biggest rental car company in North America, and arguably the world, by building a huge network of neighborhood locations, largely under the radar of its competition. Enterprise also decided to enter the airport market and continued to expand there. Despite its relatively small airport presence, the company actually tied Hertz for the J. D. Power and Associates award for client satisfaction among airport-based car rental companies in 1999. Enterprise went on to win the J. D. Power airport satisfaction award among car rental companies for eight of the following ten years.

Still, Enterprise's share of the airport market was around 8 percent in 2007 and increasing by only about one-tenth of 1 percent each month. By contrast, Alamo and National collectively had about 20 percent. Avis and Hertz together controlled around half of the airport market. Enterprise had 230 airport locations, compared to a combined 3,800 for Alamo and National. "I looked at these numbers and realized I'd be really, really old by the time we got to that kind of scale at the rate we were growing with just the Enterprise brand," Andy recalls.

How could Andy accelerate this growth? The answer came to him one day while reading an article in the *New York Times.* On February 14, 2007, the paper reported that Dollar Thrifty Automotive Group, owner of Dollar Rent A Car and Thrifty Car Rental, was in the final stages of buying Vanguard—and therefore the Alamo and National brands—from Cerberus. The private equity firm wanted to cash out on its investment in Vanguard and had considered several options, including taking the company public again. Cerberus senior managing director Lenard Tessler, who oversaw the Vanguard transaction, didn't even think about approaching Enterprise given its lack of interest in the past.

However, this time was different. Andy and his team had been studying the industry and meeting with investment bankers to better understand where the business was headed. They realized it was important to gain a stronger foothold in the airport market and were intrigued by the potential opportunities that Alamo and National would create for both customers and employees. Research showed that existing Enterprise customers were increasingly interested in doing business with the company at airports, yet its presence there was relatively small. Building additional scale on its own would take a lot of time, given that airport slots are limited and rarely come up for bid. Enterprise also had other challenges to conquering this business. For starters, it wasn't set up to serve the corporate travel market. In addition, business travelers generally want frequent-renter programs and very quick service, neither of which the company offered. Plus, Enterprise—already a low-cost provider—refused to offer the highly discounted deals sought by bargain-hunting leisure travelers. By contrast, National was known for serving business travelers and had the coveted Emerald Club frequent-renter program, while Alamo was known as a great discount brand.

Though Enterprise still had plenty of growth opportunities for employees as a stand-alone company, expanding into all of these airport locations would also accelerate the potential for up-and-coming managers to move up the ladder and increase their knowledge by learning to master some very different ways of running the business. "Key to our interest in Vanguard was the ability to create growth opportunities for employees, and this gave us a chance to do it in a different way," says Enterprise president and chief operating officer Pam Nicholson.

Andy came to the conclusion that purchasing Alamo and National would instantly give Enterprise a hugely expanded presence at airports with almost zero overlap. Overnight, the company's market share at airports would nearly quadruple. He also saw the potential to bring Enterprise's expertise in delivering exceptional customer service to two brands serving extremely different target markets. At the same time, Vanguard's custom-built technology systems would allow Enterprise to completely automate the airport rental process, something the company hadn't really needed up to this point since its business was built around serving a different customer base in a more traditional way. And given Vanguard's huge losses over the years, the purchase came with some interesting tax benefits.

PAY THE RIGHT PRICE

A fatal mistake many companies make in acquiring another company is overpaying. Before extending a formal offer, Andy had his top lieutenants run the numbers to figure out what Vanguard was worth. They also had a sense of what Dollar Thrifty planned to pay—it was revealed in the *New York Times* article. With a number in hand, Enterprise vice chairman Don Ross phoned Tessler to convince him to consider the possibility of selling Vanguard to Enterprise instead. Tessler was open to the idea and threw out a range for what he thought the business would fetch. As it turned out, the numbers matched Enterprise's internal estimates of around $3 billion of invested capital, similar to what Dollar Thrifty planned to pay. At this point, it became clear that price wasn't a problem. While the money was similar to other offers on the table, Cerberus was attracted to the fact that Enterprise could pay for the deal in cash, allowing the firm to deploy these funds right away into other investment ventures.

GET YOUR TEAM ON BOARD

Given that Cerberus was close to cutting a deal with Dollar Thrifty, the Enterprise team had to move fast. Over the next thirty days, both parties did additional due diligence. Inside

Enterprise, top executives began discussing the pros and cons of the acquisition, along with the potential logistical challenges. They initially kept such conversations to a very close inner circle and used code names in the discussions—"Marlin" for Vanguard and "Arch" for Enterprise—to keep any information from leaking to employees or the press. At the same time, Andy had side conversations with family members, including Jack, to see if they were on board with the purchase. Both the Taylor family and the Enterprise board of directors thought it was a great idea, though some on the company's senior leadership team had reservations. They agreed that the merger posed almost no financial risk, given Enterprise's pristine balance sheet and the fair price. But there was plenty to be concerned about. For one thing, Enterprise had a fleet of about six hundred thousand cars at the time, while Vanguard's was two hundred thousand strong. That in itself created a significant logistical challenge that would have to be managed. At the same time, Vanguard had nine thousand employees and some thirty-five collective bargaining units, something Enterprise never had to deal with before. Vanguard also operated under a very different and more volatile airport business model. Even those who supported the idea feared that an acquisition of this size could harm the company's unique culture. Among the concerns was whether Enterprise's entrepreneurial, college-educated management trainees would have a hard time working with the largely hourly workforce at Alamo and National.

To get a better gauge of what they might be buying, Enterprise convened what executives describe as a "double-secret" Saturday due diligence meeting at a St. Louis hotel, not far from the company's headquarters, that brought together key managers from both Vanguard and Enterprise, including Vanguard CEO Bill Lobeck. They broke up into small conference rooms and downloaded all kinds of information, from the financials to specific operational details. What surprised Enterprise most was how eager those on the Alamo and National side seemed to be about the prospect of becoming part of Enterprise.

At the end of the day, the dozen or so Enterprise executives who took part in this session huddled for dinner and unanimously agreed that what they had learned only strengthened their enthusiasm to move forward. "Everyone realized that the Enterprise brand alone could never be everything to everyone," says Nicholson. "It was a hard thing to come to grips with, but we ultimately figured out that to gain the kind of market share at airports that we have today, we'd need additional brands. It turned out that Vanguard was the perfect company to buy. The deal gave us three brands with completely different customer buckets."

SHARE YOUR PLANS BROADLY

According to research from Towers Perrin, the way a company approaches people issues in a merger or acquisition significantly impacts its chances for success. Employee-centric thinking calls for sharing your plans as soon as it makes sense, and keeping workers on both sides in the loop before and after the deal is done. Once the decision had been made to proceed with an offer, Enterprise slowly began to let others know of its plans. Initially a team of executives led by Ross gathered in locked conference rooms at Enterprise headquarters in St. Louis. They brought in a rotation of managers across various business units to begin sharing their thoughts and gathering input. Walls were plastered with jumbo-sized Post-It notes containing ideas on everything from ways disparate technology systems could be integrated to how human resources would be able to manage a very different workforce. Enterprise then held a big summit a week before the deal closed, bringing the Enterprise and National sales teams together to strategize about how they could sell the value proposition of the combined companies to big corporate accounts. "We made the decision to buy fairly quickly," Nicholson notes. "From the time we said we were interested to the day we announced the deal was around forty-five days. We had people literally working 24/7 doing the due diligence and trying to figure out what needed to be done in order to make this successful and ensure that we wouldn't be buying anything that was potentially toxic."

INTEGRATE CAUTIOUSLY

Rushing into integration and operational decisions without properly thinking them through often leads to bad results. The tendency is to merge companies in a hurry, before figuring out what you've actually purchased. The consequences of such haste can be further magnified given that you are dealing with so many moving parts. Though Enterprise was new to the acquisition game, executives had read enough case studies to know that this approach was fraught with problems.

There was a short window of just four months from when Enterprise signed the purchase agreement with Vanguard to when the deal closed. While plenty of decisions had to be made quickly, the company opted to take its time to work through logistics about everything from how to structure the combined management team to whether each brand would continue to stand on its own.

"Vanguard was set up under centralized management, which is very different from our structure," Nicholson points out. "We realized we needed to be very patient before we started making any adjustments."

One of the first decisions was appointing Greg Stubblefield, who had worked his way up from management trainee to head of all operations for California and Hawaii, to become the new president of Vanguard. Although he accepted immediately, taking the position meant moving from Southern California to Tulsa, where Vanguard was headquartered at the time. "I absolutely loved living in California and running the teams on the West Coast, so the move was kind of hard," Stubblefield admits. "But this was a tremendous challenge for me as an individual and for our business overall." Stubblefield realized his most important immediate task was to make sure the two cultures were successfully integrated.

Like the rest of the Enterprise executive team, Stubblefield joined Enterprise right out of college, in 1982. A football player with a social science degree from the University of California, Berkeley, Stubblefield was attracted to Enterprise's merit system, which we'll talk more about in a moment. For him, the approach was reminiscent of the world of sports. "The company rewarded hard work, and progression was based upon how well you did, not just years of service," he recalls. "It was about being part of a team, being willing to play any position, and being open to doing anything for the good of the business. That was appealing."

PROTECT THE CULTURE

Enterprise decided to operate Vanguard as a stand-alone business for a period of time to get to know the business and its new employees better. "The day after the deal closed on August 2, 2007, we got rid of the Vanguard name and I became president of National and Alamo, though the overall operation remained essentially unchanged," Stubblefield says. "There are several phases to an acquisition. The first is getting the deal to completion, which we did with great ease. Then you have to address all of the administrative and operations issues, which can take time to figure out. Most importantly, it's making sure you don't mess up the cultural piece."

Indeed, numerous studies show that the lack of a strong cultural integration plan is a primary reason mergers and acquisitions fail to deliver long-term value. Integrating cultures doesn't happen overnight. The cultures must be blended in a collaborative manner with constant nurturing from a leadership team that lives and breathes the values of the organization every day. To that end, one of Stubblefield's most important jobs was getting out to meet with all of the employees who were now part of the Enterprise family, to really learn how they did business and to win their hearts and minds. "We didn't want a situation where you had Enterprise guys in white shirts and ties suddenly taking over the counters at Alamo and National and saying, 'By the way, you work for me now,'" Andy Taylor says. "We made sure to treat them as equals and partners, as opposed to the vanquished or the conquered, and getting Greg out there in the field to share our culture and commitment to taking care of employees and customers was an important part of the process."

Stubblefield asked lots of questions about the history of National and Alamo, in order to understand the issues. "We didn't start any course corrections until we first thoroughly understood the business, at which point we began introducing changes in a measured and gradual way."

Even Andy spent time in the field, helping to spread the word about Enterprise's culture and commitment to employees. "I made an effort to get out to our major airport operations and shake hands with people at all levels," he says. "I met with some mechanics who hadn't had a visit from anyone in senior management in probably twenty years. What I've learned from this is you can engage people at all levels. But to do so, you have to gain their trust. Getting out to talk with them one-on-one is a very effective way to do that."

Fortunately, Enterprise found a largely receptive audience in Alamo and National employees. "We thought the acquisition was pretty exciting," says Rob Connors, a National veteran who today leads the brand marketing efforts for both National and Alamo. "We had a revolving door of leadership but knew that Enterprise only had two CEOs in its entire history, and both of them had the same last name. We also saw Enterprise growing on its own and frankly were kind of worried about them because they were expanding so much at the airport. At the same time, National and Alamo had very few home-city locations, so it seemed like a good match. I remember Bill Lobeck told all of us the day the sale closed, 'This will be the last time National is ever sold.' That was pretty comforting to everyone given all the changes up to that point."

TAKE ADVANTAGE OF SYNERGIES

Enterprise's purchase of Vanguard is a rare success story in the history of corporate acquisitions. Enterprise was a $9 billion company when it took over Alamo and National in 2007. Five years later, revenues surpassed $15 billion. Enterprise Holdings' collective airport market share continues to grow, and the purchase was quickly accretive to earnings, paying for itself within three years.

While acquisitions should not be all about synergies, it's important to take advantage of efficiencies and best practices wherever possible. Vanguard had a custom-built technology system known as Odyssey that automated the fleet management and reservation process at airport locations. Enterprise adopted and built on this system to better manage its airport operations. In addition, it rolled out its well-established customer satisfaction program (which you'll learn about in Chapter 6) across all Alamo and National locations to great effect, combined its sales teams to better service corporate accounts, integrated call and claims centers for all three brands, and adopted the best aspects of the operating models from both companies.

In the coming chapters, we'll delve into exactly how Enterprise did this, and reveal how the company trains its employees and takes care of its customers. But one of the biggest questions the company faced following the acquisition was what to do with the three brands it now owned. Should they all be merged into one? Or would keeping them separate be the better way to go? The answer came as the company began to realize how different all three brands were, and the many advantages that could bring when it came to driving loyalty across a number of unique target markets.

KEYS TO DRIVING LOYALTY BY BEING OPEN TO OPPORTUNITY

1. As you build scale, consider the many ways to move into completely different areas, provide advancement potential for employees, and serve a broader group of loyal customers.
2. While you should always be focused on organic growth and building loyalty among your primary market, be open to expanding in ways that might be outside of your comfort zone, especially when a great opportunity comes along.
3. If you decide to build scale through acquisition, avoid overpaying, regardless of how badly you want to own the other company.
4. Share your plans for growth as soon as it makes sense, so that employees at all levels are kept in the loop.
5. Protect your company's culture by ensuring that everyone in leadership lives and breathes the values of your organization every day, thus serving as an example to other employees across the organization.
6. Understand that you can engage people at all levels, but to do so, you must first gain their trust.

3 Stay True to Your Brand

When you read the following names, what thoughts and images immediately come to mind?

Tiffany & Co.
Apple
Southwest Airlines
Starbucks
Amazon.com

Without even blinking, visions of expensive jewelry probably popped into your head for Tiffany. Apple no doubt conjured up thoughts of quality and technological innovation. Southwest Airlines likely made you think about cheap air travel made possible by joke-telling pilots and flight attendants. The very hint of Starbucks probably had you smelling coffee that tasted exactly the same at every one of the company's locations worldwide. And I'll bet that Amazon brought to mind a sense of trust and the ability to buy just about anything online for less than you'd pay at brick-and-mortar stores.

Now let's take this exercise one step further. I'll give you two companies side by side. Think of what these brands mean to you, and note how they make you feel.

Nordstrom and T. J. Maxx
Chipotle and Taco Bell
Lexus and Toyota
Ritz-Carlton and Courtyard by Marriott

In each case, I'm sure you not only had specific impressions about these companies but also could instantly decipher the sharp contrasts between each pair of names. Nordstrom and T. J. Maxx both sell clothing, but the shopping experience couldn't be more different. At Nordstrom you expect high-quality merchandise and equally high prices, along with great customer service and piano music in the background as you peruse the racks. At T. J. Maxx, you know you'll find cheap prices on designer merchandise, but not much else. Before going, you anticipate the inventory will be uneven, the lines long, the crowds different from what you find at Nordstrom, and little or no personalized service. In fact, locating a clerk to help answer your question about a given item might be as tough as spotting sunshine on a rainy day.

You can fill your hunger for a burrito at both Chipotle and Taco Bell, though the overall experience is quite different. At Chipotle a burrito costs around $8, depending on what you put inside. At Taco Bell, you can get one for as little as 59¢. But for many people, paying significantly more for a burrito at Chipotle is worth it. You get a tastier end product, and you call the shots, telling the person behind the counter exactly which ingredients you want right as the burrito is being made in front of you. The atmosphere at Chipotle is also more inviting, complete with art on the walls that combines with hip music to make the overall experience feel a lot more expensive. It's what the industry refers to as the "fast casual" dining category. Fast casual restaurants don't offer sit-down service, but the overall quality is a notch above what you normally find at fast-food establishments.

Lexus and Toyota both make excellent cars. In fact, the brands are owned by the same company—Toyota. In some cases, Lexus and Toyota models are manufactured using identical parts and in the same plants. The difference is that Lexus brings to mind a sense of luxury and higher prices. Toyota, by contrast, conveys a sense of reliability, but with vehicles that are more downscale and affordable, even though you might ultimately wind up with something very similar in quality.

Likewise, Ritz-Carlton and Courtyard by Marriott are both wholly owned subsidiaries of Marriott International, but the lodging experience at these brands is very different. Both can provide a good night's rest, but you'll be surrounded with luxury and pay much higher prices at Ritz-Carlton, while Courtyard caters to more budget-minded travelers who need few frills and don't care about having an on-site restaurant, concierge, or any other of the other services one takes for granted at resorts.

Incidentally, it's not just large corporations that spend time and energy building well-recognized brands. Successful and savvy individuals do as well. Jack Welch parlayed his celebrity as CEO of General Electric to create a brand as the ultimate expert on leadership and business management. Simon Cowell used his unique personality, British accent, and fame on *American Idol* (and now *The X Factor*) to become viewed as the most credible judge of singing talent in the country. Lady Gaga (the name itself is a brand since the singer's real name is Stefani Joanne Angelina Germanotta) has built a reputation as an eccentric pop singer who is known for her flamboyance and support of humanitarian causes. Even Jets star Tim Tebow stands apart from his fellow football players with a brand as a squeaky-clean Christian, really nice guy, and dual threat on the field who can effectively rush and pass.

The fact that such specific images and thoughts about each of these companies and individuals instantly come to mind isn't a surprise. All have spent years and, in the case of most corporations, millions if not billions of dollars building their brands to become this familiar.

It's important to note that each brand discussed has been highly effective at attracting legions of loyal customers and employees by catering to a specific niche. I have some friends who shop at Nordstrom all the time but wouldn't be caught dead walking into a T. J. Maxx. I know others who swear by the great deals at T. J. Maxx and would never consider paying full price for merchandise at Nordstrom. Toyota has long been known for making reliable and fairly priced cars, and the company consistently ranks high in customer loyalty surveys. But fans of Lexus tend to make a lot more money and view this brand as being more in line with their desire for status and luxury. Why else would someone pay $9,000 more to get a Lexus ES350 instead of a Toyota Avalon, considering that both vehicles come with the exact same engine, not to mention similar body styles and other features?

Young people looking for cheap eats love Taco Bell, though the slightly older and higher-income demographic that Chipotle targets views it as being beyond compare for a quick bite. Similarly, discriminating travelers with plenty of money won't stay anywhere but Ritz-Carlton, though more practical and budget-conscious travelers consider Courtyard by Marriott to be a more than acceptable home away from home.

In order to have loyal customers and employees, you must develop a strong brand that makes it clear what your company stands for. You then have to build on your brand promise, ingrain it in your culture, market it effectively to your target audience, passionately convey the unique need you meet, and ensure that everyone in your company works with a laser-like focus every day toward the ideals you have set for this brand.

MARKET AND DELIVER AN EXPERIENCE

A solid brand is the greatest asset any company owns. At its most basic level, a brand is a promise that resides in customers' minds about what they can expect when doing business with your company. The most effective brands build an emotional relationship with customers that forms the basis of lifelong loyalty. Those who are passionate about your brand will serve as evangelists and tell others about you through a variety of means. They'll also want to do business with you all the time regardless of price. By contrast, a weak brand can have the exact opposite effect, especially in a world where, thanks to the various social media outlets available, every individual has a platform from which to shower both praise and complaints on any company.

"The value of having a strong brand cannot be overstated," says Patrick Farrell, Enterprise's chief marketing and communications officer. "Well-positioned brands provide consumers with a sense of confidence and trust in the products they choose. Strong brands enhance margins and work toward ensuring a sustainable, profitable business."

There are two primary challenges to building a brand. First, you must be able to clearly define what attributes set your organization apart from the competition. Second, you need to decide how to make those attributes come to life. This involves both traditional marketing and delivering a unique experience for those customers who do business with you. Quite often the latter can have an even greater impact, especially when you are working on a more limited budget.

"For proof, you just need to take a look at a company like Starbucks, which has only recently started to spend any money on advertising," notes Jim Stoeppler, brand director for Enterprise Rent-A-Car. "Starbucks built its brand based on delivering a great experience and having a presence on every street corner. That, quite frankly, is very similar to how Enterprise did it as well."

Building a brand involves being consistent in your delivery and remaining on point with your messaging through multiple marketing channels, a subject we'll explore further in Chapter 8.

"That was one of the smarter aspects of the previous ad campaign we had at Enterprise, which always ended with the tagline 'Pick Enterprise. We'll pick you up,' " Stoeppler notes. "People remembered that, and we delivered on the promise when they rented from us. Even though we've stopped using that campaign, when you sit in a focus group today and ask people what they think of when they hear the name Enterprise Rent-A-Car, the response is often, 'Oh, they're the company that picks you up.' And it's about more than just the act of picking customers up. This slogan came to signify what Enterprise stood for, and communicated our emphasis on service."

Successful companies are always in a mode of building, nurturing, and protecting their brand, making alterations along the way based on a changing marketplace, but never losing sight of the essential elements on which it was constructed in the first place.

Key Traits for Building a Successful Brand

To build a successful brand you must be able to define and articulate these key traits:

- **Mission**
- **Purpose**
- **Heritage**
- **Culture**
- **Personality**
- **Strengths**
- **Weaknesses**
- **Threats**
- **Primary and secondary audiences**

TAKE STOCK OF YOUR HERITAGE

During its first fifty years in business, Enterprise Rent-A-Car built its brand as the car rental company that exceeded customer expectations and delivered high-touch service, largely in the home-city markets. Picking customers up was merely one way to show this. Enterprise became the company people turned to when they needed a replacement vehicle because either their own car was in the shop or they planned a short out-of-town trip and didn't want to put miles on their personal vehicle.

By contrast, both Alamo and National were primarily based at airports, but they served different target markets. National was founded in 1947 by a group of twenty-four independent car rental operators with a collective fleet of eight hundred cars and sixty locations. National became an official corporation in 1959, establishing itself as offering "the best in localized, personal service." National went on to pioneer a number of services that were unique at the time, including the ability to select any car on the lot for one flat price. It was also the first car rental company to create a computerized reservation system, in 1966.

During the 1970s National started to focus on building its corporate account effort and became known as the premier provider for business travelers. In 1987 National launched the Emerald Club, which was the industry's first frequent-renter program. Members got to use a paperless rental agreement, which made the process of getting into their vehicle faster since all information needed to complete the transaction was already stored electronically. This ultimately morphed into the Emerald Aisle, which allowed members to select any car they wanted and get on their way without filling out any forms.

Alamo had been around since 1974 and largely served leisure customers looking for good deals. The company began with four locations in Florida and carved out a niche for being the rental car company that provided a fun, low-cost experience for vacationing families, leading to close ties with many international tour operators and a partnership with Disney.

Like National, Alamo has long relied on technology to streamline operations. It became the first car rental company with real-time booking capabilities on the Internet in 1995, and it started the first online check-in system in 2005. It also built check-in kiosks, which were placed in high-traffic locations, giving customers the chance to choose their own vehicles, request upgrades, and drive off the lot without needing the assistance of counter personnel.

The fact that all three brands served such different customers was a primary reason Enterprise was interested in buying Alamo and National. But what wasn't immediately known was whether all three brands should be merged with Enterprise or instead be allowed to continue operating as individual entities. Among the considerations was that both National and Alamo had been through numerous owners over the years, including General Motors and H. Wayne Huizenga's Republic Industries, along with a trip through bankruptcy for a few years beginning in 2001. Employees had been subjected to a revolving door of CEOs, each with a different vision for the two companies. Little had been invested in either brand for some time, since eking out earnings took a front seat to the customer experience. As a result, while both National and Alamo were still viable brands, there was some thought that turning them all into Enterprise locations might be an effective way to give National and Alamo a fresh start.

STAY IN YOUR SWIM LANE

In order to make this all-important decision, Enterprise had numerous internal discussions and brought in some outside consultants to help. "We spent a lot of time studying our options," Farrell shares. "We went over various scenarios and attempted to understand how different decisions might play out in the long run."

The company focused on three primary options: move everything over to the Enterprise brand, have just two brands—Enterprise and National—or keep all three brands in place.

"As a marketing guy, it was obvious to me that each brand had very different customers, segments, and brand promises," says John MacDonald, now Enterprise Holdings' vice president of brand marketing. "But it took us a while to figure it out, given the different opinions. One consultant felt strongly that we shouldn't keep all three brands. Even though he believed they could successfully coexist, he thought it would be too difficult for us to manage."

At the end of the day, Enterprise decided that because the

customer base was so different, keeping and nurturing three distinct brands was the most effective option for moving the business forward. After all, to the casual observer, all rental car providers look the same. The fact that you can instantly search for the lowest price among the many potential options online makes it appear to be an undifferentiated commodity. When you add in that car rental counters at the airport are all lumped together in the same place, one next to the other, making your brand stand out is even more important. The goal was to build such strong loyalty that customers went straight to one of the three Enterprise brands when they were ready to book, depending on what experience they were after. The only way to get there was by building solid recognition for each brand, a message that spoke to the appropriate target audience.

"It's really difficult for one brand to be all things to all people," Farrell says. "We originally had one product, Enterprise Rent-A-Car, which was growing at the airport but didn't compete very well for the high-end business traveler. That just wasn't our market. National essentially targeted that space. Alamo was designed for leisure travelers looking for discounts, which is very different from both Enterprise and National. After some good healthy discussion, we realized that we had the ability operationally to manage all three brands because of our size, and the right solution was to present consumers with three very distinct products, each with its own brand promise."

Keeping all three brands also made the acquisition more in line with the company's mission to put customers and employees first. "The company viewed the purchase of Alamo and National not as a way to make more money due to efficiencies and streamlined operations, but rather as a way to reach more customers in different ways," MacDonald adds. "The ability to reach and penetrate more markets was primary, and only after figuring that out did we begin to concern ourselves with how this could make the company more profitable."

Merging the fleet helped in this process, because cars could be moved around where needed. "With National, weekdays are the busiest, but it's a lot quieter on the weekends," Farrell notes. "By having one common fleet, we could move cars from National to Alamo on slow days, and vice versa."

But though the fleet is shared, the brand promise is not. In other words, the cars may be similar, but how the rental experience is delivered helps to define each brand.

While the Alamo, Enterprise, and National marketing and brand managers work in the same office and meet on a regular basis, their messaging is very different. They are careful to make sure all three brands stay in their own "swim lane," meaning they never stray from those elements that make up each brand's core competencies.

"The brand manager is responsible for being a bit of a zealot for the brand," Farrell observes. "They are passionate advocates who make sure the brand voice is properly reflected in everything we do." Each brand manager has his or her own brand bible that details how each item should be represented, from the brand's retail trade dress on down. Brand managers further make sure the voice of the brand is appropriately conveyed across all communication channels.

"We like to talk about Enterprise as being a purpose-driven brand," Stoeppler says. "We think of ourselves as the brand that moves people's lives forward by exceeding their expectations. It goes back to our original model of helping customers get back on their feet and on with their life when their own vehicle is not available for one reason or another. While the brand has expanded to now include airport and truck rentals, along with car sales, all relate to helping people move their lives forward."

"Alamo caters to the leisure traveler or vacationer who maybe rents a car once or twice a year," notes MacDonald. "Alamo customers need a bit of hand-holding to get through the process and are the least loyal since they tend to make decisions based on price. But if we are able to create a good experience for them, we hope that they'll think of us first the next time they travel."

"National customers are very frequent travelers, or business pros as we call them in our commercials," Connors offers. "They want to bypass the counter, choose their own car, and be on their way. If they need help, they expect to have somebody readily available nearby. National customers really value speed, choice, and control."

GIVE YOUR BRAND AN OVERHAUL

While Enterprise Holdings was clear about the promise of all three brands, Alamo and National weren't where they needed to be when the company took them over. "The culture at the previous owner, Vanguard, was somewhat transitory," admits MacDonald, who before the acquisition had worked in various marketing and sales roles with Vanguard since 1997. "We had brought together two brands—Alamo and National—many years earlier, but there was no real focus on what each should stand for. Management would concentrate its energy on Alamo for one month, and then the next they'd let what was happening at National drive our operational thinking. It was a very unsettled environment, with people trying a lot of different things."

Farrell says the Alamo brand had gone into a state of disrepair and was starting to lose some of the public's trust. At the same time, National locations were looking a bit run-down and were in need of a makeover. "The basics were there, but we really wanted to reinvigorate these brands," he says. "We made a commitment to invest tens of millions of dollars to do this. With National, for instance, we updated everything—the logo, the retail space, our lots, and our loyalty club credentials. For example, we developed a concept called the National Gateway that upgraded the retail space to include these beautiful canopies that make customers feel as if they are literally walking through a gateway when they enter the lot. We're trying to create an experience that gives the frequent renter what they want: a fast and easy way to get a car and, as we put it, 'go like a pro.' "

The company set out to reestablish National as a premier rental brand for road warriors by focusing on four key areas: vehicles, process, people, and facilities. National customers want a wide selection of low-mileage, well-maintained vehicles. They expect to rent their cars as quickly as possible with little or no employee interaction. That said, they still want employees to be readily available for support when needed. Plus, clear signage and the updated canopies help business travelers more easily navigate through each location.

"National's Emerald Club had a great base of loyal users but was getting few new customers," says Greg Stubblefield, Enterprise's chief strategy officer. "The brand was fading, and we wanted to bring National to the forefront so business travelers would think of it first. At the end of the day, we wanted them to understand that we do customer service, cars, and quick transactions better than the competition."

"By having three brands, we are always able to stay on point with the message and never deviate from delivering on our promises," MacDonald adds. "When it was just Alamo and National before, we sometimes strayed into the other's brand territory just to build up the business. We don't have to do that anymore. Our focus is extremely targeted."

As one example, Enterprise is gradually working to make sure the shuttle bus customers take represents just one brand—Enterprise, National, or Alamo—whenever possible. Under the old model, which was the brainchild of a cost-conscious court-appointed business manager during the time National and Alamo were in bankruptcy many years ago, the same bus was used by both National and Alamo, with the two logos painted on the outside. This move saved money, but it created a confusing message and led to a bus filled with very different types of travelers, undermining the individuality of the two brands.

To build an effective brand, you must be laser focused. When you send mixed messages in the hope of reaching everyone, you won't clearly resonate with any specific audience, including the one you most want to connect with. If your company offers an array of different services and product offerings, separating out into different brands—as Enterprise did—may be an effective way to go.

"You see one company successfully managing multiple brands

quite often in the travel industry," notes Connors. "Many hotel chains have multiple brands, because they realize the value in reaching different audiences. Hilton has ten different brands. The company has figured out that a traveler attracted to a Hilton probably won't consider staying in a Homewood Suites. The opposite is also true. If Hilton didn't have multiple brands serving different markets, another competitor would enter the space and take this business. It's hard to be all things to all people in the travel market, because everyone's ideal experience is so personal. If you don't offer multiple options, it's tough to gain a greater share of the overall business."

DELIVER ON YOUR BRAND PROMISE

What customers experience when doing business with you plays a huge role in creating your brand identity. You then have to back this up with a full-spectrum marketing initiative to tell your story to the public, as I'll explain more fully in Chapter 8. Delivering a great customer experience is something you should promote in your branding. But don't start talking about it until you've really perfected the process. There's nothing worse than overpromising and underdelivering.

Several years ago, I was hired to consult for a small regional bank that wanted to become more widely known for offering superior customer service. The bank's president realized there was nothing in place at the time to set his branches apart from the competition's. Ideally, he hoped to build a brand that conveyed to the world that his was the friendliest bank in town, in order to attract more business and increase customer loyalty. But there was a lot of work to be done. When I asked him to describe the bank's value proposition during our initial call, he replied, "We really don't have one—yet. That's why I hired you."

After learning more about the bank, and talking with both customers and other company executives, I realized there was significant potential to be unlocked.

Fortunately, the bank did a good job of hiring and largely had a customer-oriented team in place. But there was no formal training program to develop these customer service skills, employee compensation wasn't properly aligned, nothing was being measured, and the technology the bank employed felt like it came straight from the 1970s.

I explained to the president and his executive staff that in order to build the bank's brand, they would first have to commit to creating an environment that truly did have the friendliest employees in town. This involved a big investment in training and infrastructure. But it could put the bank in a position to stand head and shoulders above the competition (especially since I did some survey work revealing that the other banks in town were largely viewed as being difficult to do business with). Only after this was in place could we start to send out a message about this bank's renewed brand commitment through various marketing channels. The website, for example, needed a major overhaul. Above all, top management would have to commit to operating with this customer-first mentality as the normal course of doing business. You can't fake it. Customers must experience the brand each time they walk inside a branch or have an interaction by phone. In fact, without this last element, building an enduring brand is virtually impossible. And if there's ever a break in delivering on your brand promise, you can lose all credibility with customers—including previously loyal ones—in short order.

Consider the case of Circuit City, at one time among the nation's premier consumer electronics retailers. Founded in 1949, the company pioneered the concept of large-format superstores, carrying everything from computers to appliances under one roof. As the company's growth took off in the 1980s, Circuit City became known for three things: its trademark building design with a red protruding structure that resembled an electrical plug, low prices, and exceptional service. In fact, Circuit City built its brand on service and used the popular advertising slogan "Welcome to Circuit City, where service is state of the art."

The company had a very successful run, growing to become the second-largest electronics retailer in the United States.

By 2000, however, the company began to change its stripes. It abandoned the "plug" design in favor of storefronts that looked almost identical to archrival Best Buy. Circuit City also stopped carrying appliances, even though it sold more than any retailer other than Sears. What's more, Circuit City salespeople were once highly experienced and paid on commission. They had a huge incentive to take care of customers and earn their loyalty, since repeat business translated into a bigger paycheck. To save money, however, Circuit City converted everyone over to an hourly wage, which caused some of the best salespeople to leave. Worse, in 2007 the company cut everyone's hourly pay and laid off the highest-earning team members, who were also generally the most experienced. The result was low employee morale, which translated into a horrible customer experience. This ultimately sent Circuit City into bankruptcy and out of business. The company stands out as an abject lesson on how a brand can be destroyed by changing or eliminating the very practices that contributed to building it in the first place.

How to Build a Successful Brand and Loyal Customer Base

1. Find out what your customers need—and how your brand meets that need.
2. Identify what differentiates your brand.
3. Deliver your brand identity by using consistent messaging across all media.
4. Develop customer loyalty through solid execution.
5. Stay true to the brand's identity and mission.
6. Remain relevant.

YOUR PEOPLE ARE PART OF YOUR BRAND

Never underestimate the importance of the role those on your team play in delivering on your brand promise. In many cases, your employees may actually *be* your brand. A good case in point can be seen in the wealth management industry. There are a number of large, well-known national firms, and each has its own brand in the marketplace. However, clients generally choose to hire a firm based largely on the advisor they will be working with. Clients find advisors in many different ways, from personal referrals to ads to educational seminars. Clicking with the advisor and developing a personal bond is what often wins the client's business, even more than the firm's reputation or investment results. Yes, the fact that the advisor works for a highly regarded company is an important part of the decision-making process, but the advisor is the ultimate point person who touches the client.

Given that, if an advisor moves to another firm, there's a high probability the client will move with him or her. This means that, depending on your industry, when you lose your people, you may also lose part of your brand.

There are two important takeaways. As an individual, you should work hard to build your own personal brand; it will make you a more valuable employee and help you to build a closer bond with your customers. As a manager or business owner, you need to understand that the people who work for you are an extension of your brand, a reality that should never be overlooked.

CRAFT A CATCHY SLOGAN

One of the most effective ways to build a brand is by coming up with a catchy slogan that instantly communicates your brand's promise. It needs to be clear, concise, easy to remember, honest, and simple to understand. Consider the following examples:

Wheaties: The breakfast of champions
Miller Lite: Great taste . . . less filling
Maxwell House: Good to the last drop
Energizer: Keeps going and going
BMW: The Ultimate Driving Machine
Timex: It takes a licking and keeps on ticking
Disneyland: The happiest place on earth
Allstate Insurance: You're in good hands with Allstate
FedEx: When it absolutely, positively has to be there overnight
Enterprise Rent-A-Car: Pick Enterprise. We'll pick you up.
National Car Rental: Go National. Go Like a Pro.
Alamo Rent A Car: Drive Happy

In each case, the slogan—or brand statement—instantly describes the company's business and brand promise in just a few words, and it embodies what your brand stands for. Think about your own company. If you already have a slogan, is it short, unique, and does it properly convey your brand? Will customers instantly get what you do when they hear it? If not, how would you change it in order to connect with your customers and employees more effectively?

Your company's slogan should be used in all of your marketing efforts, since consistency and repetition are needed to build brand recognition. In the coming chapters, we'll take a look at the many ways to do this—both online and off—that are now at your disposal.

KEYS TO DRIVING LOYALTY BY STAYING TRUE TO YOUR BRAND

1. Develop a strong brand that makes it clear what your company stands for, while reaching your target market and conveying the unique needs you meet.
2. Continually build on your brand, ingrain it in your culture, market it effectively, and adhere to it with a laser-like focus every day.
3. Get customers to develop an emotional relationship with your brand, so they will become passionate evangelists for your company and tell others about it.
4. Clearly define what sets your organization apart from the competition and figure out how to make those attributes come to life.
5. Adjust your brand's key attributes based on the changing marketplace, while never losing sight of the essential elements on which it was constructed.
6. Don't try to make your brand all things to all people.
7. Identify your target markets and stay focused on delivering on your brand promises.
8. To reach multiple audiences, consider operating different brands, each with its own unique identity.
9. Appoint a brand manager to serve as a passionate advocate for the brand to ensure your company's voice is properly reflected in everything you do.
10. Communicate your brand's promise through a short, clear, easy-to-remember slogan.
11. Work hard to build your own personal brand, since employees are a key brand differentiator for most companies.

4 Engage Your Workforce

Few people grow up with dreams of working in the rental car business, particularly those who ultimately go on to earn a college degree. After all, it's not perceived to be a glamorous or particularly lucrative industry. For Enterprise, this created real challenges in the company's early years in terms of attracting highly qualified candidates to its management training program.

"Unlike other car rental companies, we were looking for bright college graduates to come join the business, and some of their parents thought their kids were crazy," recalls Enterprise chairman and CEO Andy Taylor. "They couldn't believe these men and women planned to use the expensive degree that they just spent tens of thousands of dollars on to go rent cars. Plus, we had to compete with other corporations looking for these same promising candidates."

What those parents didn't realize was that Enterprise had developed a management-training program unparalleled in the car rental industry. Founder Jack Taylor originally came up with it as a way to encourage employee loyalty and retention, while also making sure the interests of both the company and its employees were properly aligned.

TRAIN FROM THE GROUND UP

Enterprise offered bright candidates with no industry experience the chance to get paid while learning everything they needed to know about running a successful business. If they worked hard and proved their abilities, they had the potential to run their own branch office within a couple of years. And they could share in the profits of the operation as it grew, without having to put a penny of their own money at risk. The only catch was that they had to be willing to work hard and learn the company's way of doing business from the ground up.

Enterprise Rent-A-Car's management training program today is very similar to the one Jack Taylor set up nearly six decades ago. The Enterprise brand primarily recruits college graduates looking to get into a structured management training program that offers an opportunity to exercise their entrepreneurial drive. The company takes on promising candidates with degrees from a variety of majors. Often they are undergraduates. Few new hires come in with an MBA or other master's degree, which really isn't needed given the company's comprehensive business training program.

The company also looks for candidates who, by way of achievements in high school, college, and their community, have demonstrated their leadership potential, people skills, work ethic, and drive to succeed. Being an athlete is another plus, given that Enterprise prefers those who have a team spirit and like to compete.

"We look for people with what I would call a busy background," explains Matt Darrah, Enterprise's executive vice president of North American operations. "We want someone who has contributed to the cost of their education by working and who was also very involved, be it through athletics, fraternity or sorority life, a leadership position, and so forth. The specific degree is less important. What really matters is a demonstrated track record of working hard, because if you're going to be above average, you have to be willing to work harder than others."

Darrah notes that he had no interest in working for a rental car company when he started with Enterprise in 1984. Darrah earned a degree in marketing management from Mount Union College in Ohio and applied at Enterprise only because he wanted to practice his job interviewing skills. "To my surprise, I was really wowed by the Enterprise story and the chance to work as an entrepreneur," he says. "It really clicked for me that this is what I wanted to do. I started as a management trainee in Southern California and worked my way up like everyone else here over time."

CREATE AN ENTREPRENEURIAL ENVIRONMENT

Historically, roughly 95 percent of the company's new full-time hires came through the management training program. This changed a bit after the acquisition of Alamo and National in 2007. Now a good deal of the workforce is not on the management track, preferring instead to stay in the same position for many years. Dealing with this new, largely hourly workforce was a bit of an adjustment for Enterprise Holdings, as we'll soon see. But in order for an employee to move into a leadership position at any of the company's three brands, he or she has to go through the Enterprise Rent-A-Car management training program.

Trainees have a unique opportunity to rise from the ground floor to running their own network of branch locations in a matter of years. It's an entrepreneurial structure that attracts high-caliber talent.

New hires generally start out with an annual salary ranging from $33,000 to $40,000, depending on geography. Within the first twelve to eighteen months, trainees become management assistants and then assistant branch managers. Once they are in management, in addition to a slightly higher base salary, they earn a percentage of the branch's profits. After two or three years with the company, they have the potential to move into a branch manager role, which comes with an even bigger percentage of overall profits. Within five to six years, an employee can become an area manager, responsible for three or four branches, then move up to being a regional or group manager, and ultimately achieve the general manager level. Those who reach the very top of this structure have the potential to earn a seven-figure compensation package, as they receive a portion of the profits from every branch under their control.

Giving employees a chance to share in the profits of a business instills a strong sense of engagement. It makes everyone think and act like an owner, meaning they are constantly looking for ways to make the company more successful. Such employees tend to work as many hours as necessary and do whatever it takes to get the job done.

Granted, Enterprise has a unique structure that isn't easily replicated or even practical for many businesses. But the general concept of ensuring that employees are paid fairly and compensated based on profitability aligns everyone's interests and is a huge driver of loyalty.

In a way, Enterprise runs its business like a corporate-owned franchise system, with headquarters in St. Louis and literally thousands of small self-run businesses across the country. The corporation provides full support and general guidance, but it's up to each branch to run its own operation under the direction of a general manager. The general manager then reports back to a senior vice president at the corporate office. Unlike a franchise, employees don't have to invest their own money, yet their income is based on the profitability of the locations they oversee.

"All of these groups are subsidiaries of the parent with local control of day-to-day operations," says Enterprise president and chief operating officer Pam Nicholson, who also started out as a management trainee. "Even though we're a big company, we run it as a small business, giving managers full autonomy to do what they think is best in their home area."

Each individual operating group has its own budget and makes its own decisions about everything from real estate leases to how many employees to hire. The groups also get to choose which Enterprise business units beyond car rental they want to run in their area, such as fleet services, automobile sales, or truck rentals. The corporate office is relatively small, considering the company's size. Enterprise employs about two thousand people in its St. Louis headquarters, and more than half of those work in technology, which is a centralized function. Treasury, insurance, legal, marketing, and communications are also handled at a corporate level. Everything else is decentralized and run locally.

"I regard our headquarters as a massive switching station of ideas," Andy Taylor says. "At most companies, people are always looking up on high and asking, 'What do you want me to do?' We take another path. We look to our people and say, 'Do the right thing for your customers and your teams.' We let them figure it out."

When Jack was still in his twenties and working as a used car salesman at the local Cadillac dealership, he saw how motivating it was to be given both autonomy and the potential to share in a piece of the action. By taking good care of his customers, he quickly became very successful. Jack was paid a base salary of $2,000 a month and got 15 percent of the dealership's profit on his sales. In a short time he earned the equivalent of more than $250,000 a year in today's dollars, thanks to his strong ability to close deals. After five years on the job, a friend explained how leasing worked and demonstrated the financial benefits, especially for wealthier customers accustomed to driving more expensive cars.

Jack was intrigued but didn't have the money to start a leasing business on his own. So he marched in to see the owner of the Cadillac dealership, Arthur Lindburg, and proposed the following deal: if Lindburg would bankroll the up-front costs of getting the business started, Jack would run it and the two could share in the profits. Lindburg was interested but decided to have four equal partners: Jack, Lindburg, and Lindburg's two sons. He wanted Jack to have some skin in the game, so he made him contribute what he could to the venture, in this case $10,000. The rest would be considered a loan.

The deal made sense to Jack, except for one problem:

Lindburg told Jack he'd have to cut his monthly base salary in half, to $1,000, because the leasing business wasn't generating any income yet.

"I remember Dad coming home and telling us, 'I'm going to take a pay cut at work,' " says Andy, who was ten at the time. "He told us we better take good care of our clothes, since they would have to last longer, and Sunday night's regular menu of steak and lamb chops was out for a while."

But Jack wasn't worried. He was confident the leasing venture would ultimately succeed and that the profit-sharing arrangement would more than make up for the temporary pay cut. Given his entrepreneurial bent, Jack also liked the idea of running his own show.

When Jack started Enterprise, he wanted to give his employees that same feeling of ownership, with the potential to share in the company's financial success. In his view, it was the ultimate way to drive loyalty.

"If I give someone a piece of the action or a bonus based on profits, they are going to do a better job and be committed to the company every time," he says. "Now, they'll also get dinged if they have too many debts or excessive expenses, but they have a chance to do very well as they attract new customers and welcome old ones back."

Many companies try to get away with paying their employees as little as possible. Enterprise has always believed in sharing the wealth. As Jack sees it, the more employees make for themselves, the more the company prospers.

"Let's say you earn $100,000 for the business and I give you 10 percent of that as a bonus, or $10,000," he offers. "By that logic, if you make us $1 million, you get $100,000. Would I rather have you make the extra $10,000 or $100,000? It's obvious. I'd much rather pay you $100,000. The more you make, the more the business makes. Why wouldn't I want that to happen?"

PROMOTE FROM WITHIN

At Enterprise, earning such a big compensation package doesn't happen overnight. You have to start out at the bottom and be willing to do whatever it takes to move the business forward. This means that you not only rent cars but also perform all of the other functions necessary to run a small business. You become fully immersed in every aspect of the operation. That way, those reporting to you in the future know that you've been in their shoes and understand exactly what they're going through.

"This is a very important part of our customer philosophy and culture," says Andy Taylor, who also began at the bottom at Enterprise, even though his father owned the company. "By getting your hands dirty and doing a little bit of everything, you get to really understand the business and learn how to deliver good customer service. These are skills you need to be in management at any level in this company."

Andy started working in the family business after getting his driver's license at age sixteen. His first job was joining Jack on trips to repossess cars from customers who fell behind on their lease payments. As the boss's son, Andy was determined to show he could succeed based on his own abilities and hard work. To prove himself, he took on the dirtiest, most challenging jobs. After graduating from the University of Denver with a degree in business administration, Andy spent three years working at a Lincoln-Mercury dealership and leasing company in San Francisco owned by Jack's brother, Paul. After getting married, he returned to St. Louis in 1973. Andy has been at Enterprise ever since.

Under the Enterprise structure, everyone in operational management is promoted from within. Knowing that your hard work will ultimately pay off and that someone from the outside won't suddenly come in and take over a spot above you creates a more stable work environment, fosters teamwork, and reduces internal jealousies and competition. At Enterprise, you can't succeed as a manager unless you also help to make others successful. Knowing that your hard work has the potential to pay off in an upward career path that you can clearly see before you is a powerful driver of employee loyalty.

As the company grows, so do the opportunities. The integration of Enterprise, Alamo, and National, for instance, gave employees from all brands the chance to take on new and expanded roles, sometimes in new geographic locations.

Beyond straight profit sharing, there are other ways a company can share its financial success with employees. Some firms award stock options, which in theory become increasingly valuable as a company does well, thus giving workers an economic incentive to make the business more prosperous. Others offer annual bonuses based on both individual and company performance for a given year. Enterprise pays its bonuses monthly, since profitability is something that gets measured on an ongoing basis.

However the compensation program is structured, offering employees a chance to share in a company's financial success can be highly motivating, especially to hard-driving overachievers in management positions.

ENCOURAGE ENTREPRENEURIAL THINKING AND RISK TAKING

Enterprise's management training program is about more than just making money. The structure empowers employees to make decisions about how to run their own business. Enterprise gives employees the freedom to experiment and stretch themselves without the fear of failure.

"Anytime you're in an environment like this, there's a lot of trial and error involved," admits Enterprise chief strategy officer Greg Stubblefield. "Early in your career, you are essentially allowed to be the owner of your own branch. You are thrust into a huge responsibility and have to be willing to try new things all the time."

Executives know that mistakes often lead to lessons that turn into great ideas. Employees are continually encouraged to tinker with new ways to run the operation and take care of customers, knowing that the company likely won't lose much even if the endeavor completely blows up. Enterprise realizes that responsibility and opportunity are like oxygen to those with an entrepreneurial spirit.

If a new innovation works at one location, it has the potential to benefit every other branch as well. "If a certain operating group comes to us and says they've found a better way to make a cheeseburger, so to speak, we'll ask for a taste of it," Andy Taylor says. "If it's good, we'll take it to other places and test it further. If it works and we are able to roll it out across the system, the results can be amazing."

This is in line with Andy's desire to keep the entire business in balance in four core areas: customer service, employee development, growth, and profitability. When any one area is off-kilter, it can hurt the bottom line. That's why branches and groups continuously turn to one another for the best practices to improve operations across the entire organization. A surprising number of these innovations result from experimentation and risk taking.

When an employee puts his or her best foot forward to try something new that doesn't work out, blame is never assigned. Sure, you need to ascertain that people have learned a lesson in the process, but it's equally important not to tell them they are personally responsible for something that didn't work out as hoped.

The idea of embracing risk taking and not condemning—or even celebrating—failure can be very motivating to a team. Jeff Stibel, serial entrepreneur and CEO of Dun & Bradstreet Credibility, has taken this concept a step further. Stibel set up a "failure wall" at his company's Malibu headquarters. He encourages employees to use a Sharpie to write about their biggest failures, both at work and otherwise. The idea, he says, is that we learn much more from our failures than we do from our successes. The wall is a way to encourage team members to take calculated risks without the fear of retribution. The concept is also incorporated into employee reviews. Workers are asked to discuss some of the ways they have failed during the year and then are assessed based on the success of those failures.

There's only one requirement that Jack asks of Enterprise employees when it comes to making mistakes: don't try to cover them up. Enterprise vice chairman Don Ross, who started out as a management trainee in the 1960s, learned the importance of this firsthand when he worked under Jack as a general manager in Kansas City. "Every Tuesday, I'd get a call from Jack and our then-CFO to discuss what was happening with the business," he remembers. "One day they wanted to talk about a lease I made for a Suburban, which was a pretty expensive car even in those days. Jack was trying to figure out how I arrived at the reported profit figure. I began adding the numbers and realized I forgot to include the interest cost in the deal, which meant we sold it for essentially no profit." Ross asked Jack what he wanted him to do. The response? "He said he didn't want me to do anything; he just wanted to hear me admit the mistake. He told me another manager had made a similar mistake and it took him ninety minutes to get the guy to admit he had done something wrong. Jack said my honesty is what he was after, and he was pretty sure I had learned my lesson and wouldn't make the same error again."

CREATE A VALUES-BASED CULTURE

Above all, for a company to engender employee loyalty it must create a culture committed to this objective. It starts with having a set of values that everyone is clear about and that those at the highest levels of the company live and demonstrate each day. Values give employees a vivid sense of what the organization stands for, show what management believes, and serve as guideposts on which all strategic decisions should be based. "Core values are like a rallying point for your organization," Andy Taylor points out. "If you choose them wisely and thoughtfully in the context of all your stakeholders, it will protect your reputation, make your employees feel good about you and your organization, and give customers a positive feeling about your company."

Core values transcend economic cycles, management changes, technological advancements, and the ever-fluctuating marketplace. They represent the beliefs and ideals everyone in the organization holds dear. Core values shouldn't be confused with slogans or catchphrases. Rather, they are what guide every move and form the primary rallying point for employees to get behind.

"Lots of companies say they are into taking care of customers and employees," Andy Taylor observes. "Trouble is, they don't live it through their core values. By standing behind your values and sticking to them, you have a chance to stand out from everyone else in today's competitive environment."

In the early days, founder Jack Taylor made sure that the company promulgated Enterprise's core values. But as the business grew, executives realized they needed to codify these principles in a more formal way. Senior management decided to have them written down and printed on a wallet-sized card given to every employee to keep in his or her pocket at all times.

Enterprise refers to its core values as "founding values" because they capture the beliefs of Jack himself. The eight founding values shown on page 56 serve as a cultural compass, defining and driving everything at Alamo, National, and Enterprise.

"These represent the values the Taylor family has been living since the company was founded. Having them printed on a card serves as a reminder for all of our employees to see every day," Andy Taylor says. "But I want to emphasize it's not just about writing this stuff down. You have to live these values and talk about them with employees all the time. Great companies clearly and consistently communicate their values and build them into the fabric of the organization. When everyone operates from the same set of guiding principles, they become a behavioral compass and your odds of continued success increase a hundredfold."

Many executives credit the company's decision to carefully articulate these founding values to Alamo and National employees following the acquisition as a primary reason Enterprise was able to extend its culture to all three brands so quickly.

FOUNDING VALUES FOR ALAMO, NATIONAL, AND ENTERPRISE

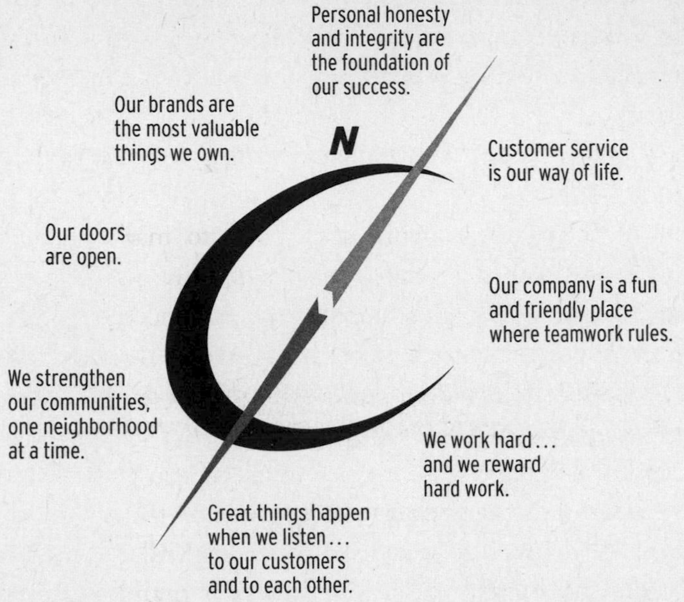

Personal honesty and integrity are the foundation of our success.
Our brands are the most valuable things we own.
N
Customer service is our way of life.
Our doors are open.
Our company is a fun and friendly place where teamwork rules.
We strengthen our communities, one neighborhood at a time.
We work hard... and we reward hard work.
Great things happen when we listen... to our customers and to each other.

"One way we did this was by assigning long-tenured Enterprise employees to work at Alamo and National locations right away, not to take over, but to share our philosophy and culture," Stubblefield says. "We also had Andy Taylor, Don Ross, Pam Nicholson, all the top folks out there articulating the exact same message. We knew we couldn't transfer the culture overnight, but we continually articulated it and then let them see how we lived these founding values, and it made a huge difference."

SET REALISTIC EXPECTATIONS

Today Enterprise gets around three hundred thousand applications annually from those eager to be part of the management trainee program and run their own rental car business. Though the company is happy to share stories about the compensation potential, it makes sure to set proper expectations, since advancement up the management ladder is a steep climb that few make all the way to the top.

"Most candidates come in thinking about where they'll be over the next twelve to twenty-four months, which is why we're careful to explain that this is a company they can be with for a long time," Nicholson says. "But they need to understand what's realistic in the short term. The last thing we want to do is overpromise."

In other words, while it's critical to make a compelling offer, you should never commit to anything you won't be able to deliver on. Engaging employees means meeting—or, ideally, exceeding—their expectations. If they come in expecting something greater than what you can actually provide, it will create resentment and lead to disengagement. It's also important to remember that a promise is a promise. If you agree to a certain pay structure before an employee starts on the job, you should never be tempted to withdraw it. Nothing will drive an effective worker away from your company faster than the feeling that your company breaks its promises. Once a promise is broken, you lose all credibility from that point on and employees will stop believing anything you say.

By keeping its promises and delivering on its commitments, Enterprise has racked up an impressive 75 percent retention rate for its full-time workforce, the best in its industry. The highest turnover typically takes place in the first year, when candidates determine whether this is a good fit for them. The job isn't right for everyone, and sometimes employees don't know that until they've actually had a chance to live it. By the time an individual gets to the branch manager level, retention rates hover near 80 percent. For area managers, that number jumps to nearly 90 percent. In the executive suite, retention tops 95 percent. In terms of part-time workers, Enterprise has a retention rate of 57 percent, which may not sound impressive, but part-time turnover numbers often top 100 percent in many companies, as this workforce typically is transient by nature.

"I think the fact that you have guys like me who have been

here for so long and worked our way up helps to demonstrate to others that the potential is there to really move up in the business," Ross says. "The system does work and the growth opportunities are even greater today than when I started, despite how far the company has come. But we want people to understand that it can take time to move up the ladder."

How Enterprise Drives Loyalty Among New Hires

1. It hires only the best candidates, even when tempted to lower standards during times of high employment.
2. It is very clear in explaining the job and expectations for advancement.
3. It communicates the company's mission and gives examples of how that applies to what employees do every day.
4. It offers new employees a big-picture look after ninety days to solidify their views of what the company offers.
5. It makes sure to use the company's philosophy of "customers and employees first" as a guide when running the business.
6. It focuses on employee training, development, and mentorship.
7. It explains the importance of starting at the bottom and working your way up.
8. It celebrates and recognizes every employee, branch, and group success, while making a big deal about promotions.
9. It is honest with workers and always lets them know where they stand.
10. It listens to employees and shows how the company has implemented and acted upon their feedback.

11. **It promotes managers who lead by example and convey a positive message about where the company is going.**
12. **It never accepts anything less than excellence.**

TRAIN FROM THE GROUND UP

Being immersed in the Enterprise culture starts on day one. After being hired into the management training program, employees are assigned to a branch office and go through a business boot camp of sorts, which has been called a "virtual MBA without the IOU." The training focuses on six key core competencies: leadership, sales and persuasive skills, flexibility, work ethic, customer service ability and empathy, and communication.

Over the course of eight to twelve months, through a series of classes and on-the-job sessions, employees learn about everything from ways to deliver excellent service to managing profit-and-loss reports, controlling expenses, dealing with personnel issues, setting goals, coaching, and time management. They also work behind the counter, experiencing firsthand what it takes to run the business and meet the needs of customers.

While there are people dedicated to washing and preparing cars in most branches these days, management trainees may still have to help get cars ready and perform what might be regarded as grunt work when necessary. At the same time, they handle complaints, resolve problems, and make crucial decisions. In turn, they learn day-to-day business skills while getting to practice and refine their business know-how in real-world situations.

Primary training ends with a management qualification interview known as "the grill." Trainees face a regional or group manager who peppers them with questions about every aspect of the business. This exam is intended to be a challenging experience, since managers want to see how much employees have learned and determine how well they handle themselves under pressure. It serves as a good indication for how trainees might perform in a real-world situation and helps to separate those with true management skills from those better suited to remain individual contributors.

The Value of Interns

Enterprise Rent-A-Car hires more entry-level college graduates than any other company in the United States, with about eight thousand openings per year. Enterprise recruiters like to see a mix of extracurricular activities, community involvement, and a commitment to hard work, along with strong academic performance. The company also brings on eighteen hundred interns each summer, mostly promising college juniors and seniors. Recruiters who originally find the interns are responsible for keeping in touch with them as they finish their college studies. They communicate through regular emails, phone calls, and lunch meetings. Some even send care packages at exam time, to let the interns know the company is thinking about them. All of this attention pays off: about half of these interns wind up becoming full-time employees.

MONEY ISN'T EVERYTHING

While money is an effective way to instill loyalty, it's only one part of the equation. Following the acquisition of Alamo and National, Enterprise inherited thousands of hourly workers who were never part of any kind of profit-sharing program. Many of these employees were perfectly content being paid a fair and steady wage to work behind the rental counter, service cars, or perform any number of other essential functions. They were driven by factors much different from those motivating employees on a path toward management.

"We had built an organization full of bright and hungry people that wanted to progress and be the kings and queens of their world someday," Darrah observes. "What we learned through the integration of Alamo and National is that not everyone is built that way. Lots of people don't want the pressure. They don't want to work long hours or have all of the other stressors that are generally connected with managing a business."

This realization taught Enterprise executives that employees aren't always driven by the same motivating factors. "We had built this very successful company on a model of hiring people who were cut out to be entrepreneurs, and that was still a very effective way to grow our team of managers," says Stubblefield. "But we realized that you can also have a great workforce outside of the management ranks that is very engaged as well. When I took over as president of Alamo and National, I went out and met with people who had been working at the front counter for twenty-plus years. In the old Enterprise world, if you had told me you were at the front counter for even two years I'd have thought something was a little wrong. However, we learned that we could build loyalty across two sides: those who wanted to be in a leadership position and were driven by the opportunity to be financially successful and build their own business, and those who were perfectly content in hourly jobs doing work they really enjoyed."

For those hourly employees, motivation came in other forms, though compensation was certainly still important. That's why Enterprise set up a new structure for hourly workers that provides additional financial incentives based on productivity. While starting wages are at or slightly below the competition's, Enterprise strives to make its overall pay package for hourly employees better than what they could earn elsewhere, if they perform well on the job. "If you're really going beyond the call of duty and taking care of customers and other members of your team, we put together plans to place more money in your pocket," explains senior vice president of human resources Ed Adams.

Tips for Creating an Effective Incentive Program

1. Align incentives with company business goals and the mission of exceeding customer expectations.
2. Clearly communicate the requirements for earning the reward.
3. Allow every employee to participate at all levels of the business.
4. Offer effective rewards that will inspire your team to reach for the highest level of performance.
5. Ensure the program has a measurable return on investment, and regularly monitor its effectiveness.

UNDERSTAND THE MOTIVATING FACTORS

Regardless of how much you pay, an employee won't stay connected to the organization for long unless other motivating factors are also present. People don't want to work in an environment where they're unhappy, even if they are being paid well.

Effective managers identify the factors that serve to motivate each individual, and then take the necessary actions to drive engagement. Examples of motivating factors include providing new opportunities, establishing performance rewards, and giving recognition. Indeed, statistics show that 79 percent of people leave their jobs because they don't feel properly recognized or appreciated by their managers. Engaged employees believe they are part of something bigger than themselves and have a greater purpose in life.

The overall goal is to create a motivating culture where employees *want* to perform, not where they *have* to perform. It is your responsibility as a leader to do what it takes to create such a culture, while recognizing that what makes work enjoyable for your employees may be different from what drives you to come into the office every day.

MOTIVATING FACTORS	DEMOTIVATING FACTORS
A friendly place to work	Inappropriate behavior
Efficient processes	Lack of organization or structure
Goal alignment	Lack of expectations or performance
Trust	Lack of feedback
A sense of accomplishment	Not understanding why a task is important
Appreciation—verbal and in writing	Lack of acknowledgment
Support and encouragement	No consequences for poor behavior

ONE SIZE DOESN'T FIT ALL

Enterprise's program to instill motivation is built around two beliefs. First, people ultimately decide on their own whether they are motivated to do something. Second, what is motivating to one person may not mean much to another. For some, earning an award for a job well done may be the most exciting thing in the world. To another, this may be viewed as trivial; he or she may prefer higher compensation or a different title instead. The bottom line is that a single form of motivation won't work for everyone on your team. As a leader, you need to be aware of the different ways to motivate and reward your employees and alter your approach accordingly.

"A huge part of it relates to the employee's mind-set," Stubblefield shares. "We all start at different spots and have varying factors that develop who we are. Some people are motivated by having a safe, stable, and secure position. They don't want to move around regardless of how much they are paid. Others are primarily focused on money. These people will relocate anywhere as long as they are highly compensated. Still others are more concerned about having a good title, since they worry about prestige.

"When I was out meeting with National employees after the acquisition, I ran into this guy who had been washing cars for seventeen years," Stubblefield recalls. "He was probably in his late thirties. He told me how much he loved what he did, and assured me he was the best service agent we had in the whole company. That made me happy to see. He was motivated simply by knowing he was great at his job."

The chart below can help you to better understand and react to the motivating factors of employees on your team. For instance, if some people are motivated by learning new skills, look for ways to help the workers expand their knowledge and follow up to make sure they are able to apply these new skills to their job. Or if you have a competitive team that likes to win, stage a series of formal and informal competitions.

ACTIONS FOR INSTILLING MOTIVATION	
MOTIVATING FACTORS	**HOW YOU CAN INSTILL**
Appreciation	Say thank you privately and publicly Acknowledge when an employee helps out
Helping others	Recognize employees who assist customers and fellow workers Provide opportunities to help others
Winning	Stage formal and informal competitions
Learning new skills	Offer opportunities to learn and use new skills, through training and other programs

MOTIVATING FACTORS	HOW YOU CAN INSTILL
Learning new skills (cont'd)	Follow up to see how the skills have led to success
Being a designated leader	Provide opportunities to lead and take responsibility
Promotions	Discuss promotion criteria Detail advancement steps when offering feedback
Peer respect	Create a team with complimentary skill-sets Share positive feedback others have provided
Challenging work environment	Constantly assign new and more difficult tasks
The work itself	Talk frequently and positively about the work
Having fun	Create competitions and team-oriented activities
Working with people the employee enjoys	Create opportunities for frequent get-togethers
Solving problems	Delegate problems for the employee to tackle
Sense of accomplishment	Assign projects that stretch an employee's skills Acknowledge successes
An individual's internal standards	Be complimentary of high performance
Achieving challenging goals	Assign increasingly more difficult tasks Set S.M.A.R.T. goals
Manager's interest in employees as people	Take time to get to know your people Ask about their families and outside interests

HOLD CONTESTS TO RECOGNIZE AND REWARD

Contests, competitions, and related incentive programs are a way to combine different motivators—such as winning, fun, accomplishment, and achieving goals—and can be a powerful way to drive employee loyalty. Just remember that in addition to rewarding the winners, it's important to use such opportunities to coach and support those who don't do as well. Events designed to offer some kind of recognition should not only acknowledge top performers but also set the standard for others to meet or surpass going forward.

"We're really big when it comes to recognition," Adams says. "We do a lot of formal events, including our national meetings, where exceptional employees are honored and get a chance to shake hands with our CEO and other company officers. But we also send out emails when people get promoted." In those emails, the company not only recognizes the worker moving on to a new role but also thanks those who were involved in developing the employee, since Enterprise believes progress comes from being part of an effective team. "Sending out an email of thanks is very simple and costs nothing, but it can really boost an employee's morale," Adams adds.

Stubblefield's experience with the National service agent was among the inspirations for launching the company's annual Clean Car Championship. This event pits some of the best and fastest car cleaners in the country against one another in a friendly competition. The service agents clean and refuel nearly eight million vehicles a year. Local contests are held in branches around the country to see who can most quickly and efficiently check vehicle fluids and tire pressure, vacuum floors, and clean windows and glove boxes. Finalists are selected out of an initial field of two thousand and flown to Orlando, where they compete to take home one of three top prizes: a gold medal and $1,000, a silver medal and $500, or a bronze medal and $250. The awards are usually handed out directly by Pam Nicholson, who travels to Florida for the event.

In this particular contest, each agent has just forty-five minutes to wash and refuel two sedans and one SUV in line with the company's vehicle cleanliness and maintenance standards.

"We created this event in 2008 to highlight the importance of having clean cars, but also to emphasize the critical work our service agents do to make sure customers are completely satisfied with the rental experience," Andy says.

Another popular program is the Jack Taylor Founding Values Award, which goes to those groups that best exemplify each of the company's founding values. "We use this as a way to drive home that these values are important for everyone to think about all the time," notes Ross. "It's about staying close to our roots and reminding people of what we stand for."

"Getting awards around here is a huge deal," Nicholson says. "For many, it means more than having a bigger paycheck. For most folks it has to do with pride. The majority of your waking hours are spent at work, and you want to be proud of what you are doing and the company you work for. Contests are one way to let employees show off their pride."

Enterprise conducted research several years ago to determine the primary characteristics of its most successful management trainees. The company found that a significant number referred to themselves as "recognition junkies." It turns out that high performers in particular like to be praised and recognized, to validate the work they are doing. This sentiment was especially prevalent among members of Generations X and Y. Those in Generation Y, the so-called millennials, are driven largely by a feeling of being valued. They are constantly trying to learn and develop, and want to feel as if they are making a difference in the world. While this is also important to older workers, Enterprise's research revealed that the baby boomers in particular were more interested in being promoted for doing the best job possible. Still, recognition was very motivating and encouraging to them as well.

Why not find new and ongoing ways to recognize your employees by coming up with a potential contest that could be created for your company? Contests should be crafted to motivate your team while also helping to improve your business in the process. The planning tool below is used by Enterprise and may help to stimulate some ideas for a friendly competition of your own.

CONTEST PLANNING TOOL

Contest goal: ______________________________

Business benefit: ______________________________

Number of winners possible: ❑ One winner only
❑ Multiple winners

Time frame: ______________________________

Actions required for winning: ______________________________

____

Contest rules: ______________________________

____

Reward for winning: ______________________________

____

Again, don't forget to acknowledge the runners-up as well. While those who finish first usually get all the glory, recognizing those who put in a strong effort is also important. In the Clean Car Championship, the top three winners get a prize. But maybe you could acknowledge the top ten finishers, depending on how many people participate. What you want to avoid is staging a contest that sows seeds of discord. Certainly give the greatest plaudits to those who do best. But never fail to recognize everyone, so that they will see the support and continue to excel and push for greater results next time.

Also keep in mind that any contests or recognition events should be consistent. If you are going to start an employee-of-the-month program, for instance, be sure to recognize someone new each and every month. If you do it for just one month and then skip some time before the next award is handed out, it will appear as if you are favoring certain employees over others, and you won't build any momentum among your team.

CREATE A FUN ENVIRONMENT

Contests are an additional way to instill a feeling of fun in your culture. Even today when Jack visits an Enterprise office and talks with employees, he always asks, "Are you having fun?" And he gets very concerned when he hears anything but a resounding yes.

Enjoying what he did for a living was always very important to Jack, especially given his grueling experiences in the war. From day one he wanted to create a culture at Enterprise where every employee woke up excited about going to work.

"I honestly feel that people who enjoy their work do a better job and feel a much higher level of loyalty toward the company," Andy Taylor says. "You become engaged at a much deeper level. It's almost a spiritual sort of thing, and I'm not an overly spiritual guy. I tell people that occasionally you're going to have a bad day at Enterprise. You might even have a bad week. But if you have that over and over again, please don't come to work. You really should leave. I've been there before. At my first job out of college, I looked in the mirror every morning for six months and did not want to go back to work. It's a terrible feeling. Probably one of the main reasons I came back to Enterprise in 1973 was because it was a fun place to be."

Having fun is about creating an atmosphere where people enjoy coming to work and are willing to do anything for you, your customers, and the company. It's the ultimate form of engagement. An environment steeped in fun and creative energy is contagious. Even your customers will be able to feel it.

Think of some ways that you can inject fun into daily tasks at your office. Among the ways Enterprise does this is by having informal competitions among various branches regarding satisfaction, profitability, or growth. If one group loses to another, they might have to pay up by doing something such as cooking the winning group a steak dinner. Events like this serve as a way for Enterprise employees to build camaraderie and strengthen their ability to effectively work together as a unified team. It's also a method for forging new friendships and making everyone's job more enjoyable.

MATCH EMPLOYEES WITH MENTORS

It makes sense that Enterprise, which prides itself on promoting from within and training its own, strongly believes in the power of mentoring to develop and retain top talent. The company launched a formal mentoring program in 2007 to help develop future leaders, improve retention, increase diversity among the management ranks, and boost employee satisfaction. The program typically pairs a more seasoned manager with a more junior employee who has been at the company for at least a year. The pair meet face-to-face on a monthly basis, work through a suggested curriculum, and hold quarterly coaching sessions during the twelve-month partnership.

"We really want people to match up with mentors who can help them the most," Stubblefield says. "For instance, if you want to learn how to improve in the area of customer service, we will match you with someone who is great at improving satisfaction. Or if you need to get better at sales, we'll put you with our best salesperson. You want these people to share their knowledge so that you can become a more well-rounded businessperson."

The mentoring program's statistics validate its success. In terms of retention, 95 percent of all Enterprise mentees have historically remained in the business over rolling twelve-month periods following completion of the program, which is 20 percent higher than retention rates for Enterprise employees overall.

It's estimated that 70 percent of Fortune 500 companies offer some type of mentoring program. Implementing a program in your company will help you to develop future leaders, improve morale, and increase productivity.

Here are some things to keep in mind as you structure a mentoring program:

1. Define your goals before you start.
2. Give employees a reason to participate, but don't force it on them.
3. Match employees with the mentors who are most likely to help them reach their goals and strengthen weaker skill sets.
4. Make sure there's something in it for the mentors, too.
5. Create a structure, so mentors know exactly what they are supposed to do.
6. Track the progress of all participants, to ensure that the program is providing the desired results.

CRAFT ATTRACTIVE BENEFITS

Who wouldn't want to have a private chef cook breakfast, lunch, and dinner for them at work? Or get on-site haircuts and medical care paid for by the company? If you're lucky enough to land a job at Google, this isn't just a fantasy. It's a daily reality for every employee. Google founders Sergey Brin and Larry Page discovered long ago that providing such benefits keeps workers at the office longer, makes them happier, and leads to incredibly strong loyalty, even in Silicon Valley, where the war for talent is fierce. It's also a big recruitment tool and helps to significantly enhance productivity.

The perks at Enterprise don't quite match up to Google's, but the company does offer an attractive benefits program that includes generous paid time off, insurance, a 401(k) and profit-sharing plan, the ability to rent and purchase vehicles at a discount, and the use of a car once you reach a certain level in management. Employees also get discounts at a variety of retailers in North America.

Small gestures beyond the norm have a huge impact on driving loyalty. For instance, ordering in lunch for your team on days when people put in extra effort to get the job done can be a powerful motivator. So can handing out free movie passes or tickets to a local theme park on occasion, just to let employees know you are thinking about them.

Next to money, time off is a benefit employees value very highly. Some companies give employees an additional week of vacation after hitting certain anniversary milestones, such as five and ten years, or perhaps throw in an extra day off during one's birthday month. Chicago-based Red Frog Events takes this perk to the extreme. The company hires only candidates who agree to start out by doing a minimum three-month internship. Once you're in the door, you are entitled to unlimited vacation days. As long as your work gets done, Red Frog doesn't care how much time you take off. Other unique perks include a birthday massage, free meals for those working after 7:30 p.m., a $100 office decor allowance, and a paid sabbatical to South America, Europe, Asia, or Africa every five years.

THE FIVE FACTORS OF ENGAGEMENT

While many of the steps to foster engagement that we have discussed thus far seem pretty simple—and they are—most companies don't make an effort to instill them in the overall culture. That's why employee loyalty overall is so low. Several studies suggest that only 30 percent of employees are actively engaged in their jobs, while the rest are either not engaged or actively disengaged. The importance of engagement cannot be overstated. *Engaged* employees work with passion, are healthier, feel a profound connection to the company, drive innovation, are interested in the business, are motivated to perform, want to move the company forward, and are more likely to deliver excellent customer service. *Disengaged* workers, by contrast, often put in their time without energy or passion, essentially sleepwalking through their day. Workers who are *actively disengaged* not only are unhappy but may be busy acting out their frustration in the workplace and even undermining what engaged employees are trying to accomplish. Actively disengaged workers are estimated to cost the U.S. economy around $350 billion a year in lost productivity.

Enterprise recognizes that five primary factors drive employee engagement:

- A strong relationship with one's manager
- Clear communication of expectations and goals
- The right materials, resources, equipment, and information to achieve desired outcomes
- A manager who encourages personal and professional development
- A system where top performance is recognized

Engaged employees feel that their manager shows as much interest in them as in the business overall, and they have a clear understanding of their role on the team.

Why are engaged employees so important to your company? They are more productive, connect better with customers and referral sources, and are likely to stay with you longer. Engaged employees are also important to you as a manager, since they are more willing to help you achieve your goals, are easier to train and manage, and provide consistency in running the business. Employees themselves also benefit from being engaged: they feel good about what they do, take pride in their contributions to the company, know that they are growing, and come away with a sense of being valued.

LISTEN TO YOUR EMPLOYEES

The best way to learn what matters most to those on your team and to better understand how they feel is by asking them. Managers should always be collecting and responding to feedback as a regular part of their job. But formalizing this through an official survey that goes out to the entire population is equally important.

Every two years, Enterprise conducts an employee opinion survey, asking each individual to rate the company on a range of issues, including development and training, goals and responsibilities, ethics and social responsibility, teamwork, recognition, immediate supervisor, training and development, career orientation, management, promotional opportunities, and pay. The survey is conducted online by an outside organization, to maintain complete impartiality and confidentiality.

Once the results are in, they are communicated to the workforce along with specific actions that executives are taking in order to address any issues that emerge from the responses. "We actively look to put the ideas we get through these surveys into practice," Nicholson says. "We take the feedback very seriously because creating an environment where our employees feel valued and see opportunities for career growth only serves to make our collective organization stronger."

This commitment to truly listening and responding accordingly leads to a much higher response rate, not to mention more honest answers. In Enterprise's last survey, 94 percent of all employees participated. The average for most companies is 60–75 percent.

"Employees believe that they are being listened to, and that's a large part of engagement," Adams says. "While we can't put every single idea that's suggested into practice, we always listen to the issues put forward and look for ways to address them."

Here are some principles to keep in mind when it comes to putting together your own survey, whatever your business or industry:

1. Consider using an outside company, so employees feel you are being completely objective.
2. Keep the questions to a minimum, but be sure to cover all of the key areas.
3. Allow for open-ended responses at the end, so employees are free to say exactly what's on their mind and address any concerns that aren't covered by the standard questions.

4. Tell employees why you are conducting the survey and what you hope to get from it.
5. Be fully transparent with the results and don't sugarcoat the bad stuff.
6. Share an action plan for changes you plan to implement as a result of the feedback. (If you keep results a secret or gloss over suggested areas of improvement, workers will feel as if their constructive comments went into a black hole, and they will view the effort as a waste of time.)

EMBRACE DIVERSITY

Maintaining a diverse workforce is important for businesses operating anywhere in the world today. This means ensuring that you provide equal opportunities to people regardless of race, gender, age, or sexual orientation. It also involves welcoming a wide range of thinking and viewpoints. Enterprise sees diversity as an advantage that helps to drive loyalty for both customers and employees. The company tries to make sure that employees at each branch office mirror the local community.

Furthermore, research shows that diversity can have a positive impact on the bottom line. It brings a multiplicity of ideas and approaches to dealing with goals and solving problems. In a service business, having a diverse workforce makes it more likely that you will be able to recognize and respond to the needs of a varied customer base. This stands to reason, since customers are typically more comfortable dealing with people they can relate to.

"What surprises some is that 86 percent of car purchase decisions are made by women, so having a diversified sales team is but one way diversity is very good for our business," Adams notes.

Enterprise doesn't set any specific quotas in terms of diversity. The goal is to make sure the people in the branches speak the same language, literally and figuratively, as their customers. Companywide, about 45 percent of Enterprise's new hires are members of a minority group, while women make up about 40 percent of the overall full-time workforce.

Recruitment teams at Enterprise actively look for ways to increase the diversity of the workforce, as every company should. It only makes sense given current demographic trends. Projections indicate that by 2050, minority groups will make up more than half of the U.S. population. Similarly, almost 20 percent of Canadian citizens are foreign born, while the proportion of those living in the European Union but born outside of it is around 7 percent and rising. By embracing diversity, you will be in a better position to serve the needs of these emerging groups.

"Diversity ties back to our founding value that our doors are open," Andy Taylor says. "This commitment extends to every customer and vendor as well. We work with a diverse range of suppliers and we welcome a range of ideas and different ways of doing things."

Andy notes that Jack was ahead of the curve in terms of diversity long before others started to talk about it. "I went to a private high school and at one point a person of color decided to enroll," Andy recalls. "One of the trustees tried to stop the student from being admitted. My father and mother, along with other parents, weren't about to let that happen. They believed everyone should be treated the same. They voted to make sure the student had the right to enter the school, and today he is a physician in St. Louis."

"The world ahead of us is going to be even more diverse than it is today," adds Ross. "If you aren't looking for things to do in your company to excel in the area of diversity, you are bound to fall behind."

GIVE BACK

Statistics show that 87 percent of employees who work at companies with a philanthropic commitment have a stronger sense of loyalty. At the same time, 73 percent of customers say they are more loyal to businesses that support the local community. The

Taylor family on its own has become one of the world's biggest philanthropists. "Quite honestly, when you get so much, you ask why you are entitled," Jack admits. "I'm having a great time giving money away to things that will improve our communities; our important civic, cultural, and educational institutions; and, as a result, our world."

A number of years ago, the company decided to come up with a way to help give back to charities supported by Enterprise employees, customers, suppliers, and others connected to the company by starting the Enterprise Holdings Foundation. The company sets aside 1.25 percent of companywide pre-tax profits to fund this endeavor.

"Philanthropic giving is a normal part of doing business, and it's important that we give back in the communities that have supported our business," says Jo Ann Taylor Kindle, Jack's daughter and the president of the Enterprise Holdings Foundation. "We believe our charitable efforts make us a visible neighbor, a preferred employer, and a responsible corporate citizen, which can improve our company's performance, morale, and reputation."

Any employee can suggest a charity and request a contribution, which gets reviewed by the foundation board when it meets three times a year. Employee requests are almost always granted, assuming the charity they want to support is a recognized nonprofit organization, although the amount of the donation can vary.

"Our average gift is between $2,500 and $5,000," Taylor Kindle says, noting that the foundation has given away more than $200 million since it began. "Having a foundation is a great way to tell employees that you also want them to get involved in helping their neighbors. We tie it back to our founding values. It's our way of saying we are here to help support them in this effort."

Knowing that your employer is willing to support the same organizations you are passionate about creates a very high level of engagement and loyalty, while also promoting your company's values and standing within the community.

HIRE SMART

The process of building engagement and loyalty begins long before an employee is on board. You first need to hire smart, so that you bring into your company people who are a good fit and more likely to be engaged. An effective way to identify such candidates is by using behavioral interview techniques during the initial screening process.

How many times have you been on an interview and heard the following questions: "Tell me about yourself." "Where do you see yourself in five years?" "Why are you interested in this job?" These are among the most common questions everyone asks when meeting a candidate for the first time. Sure, the answers to these basic questions may give you some insight into who the person is, but they won't necessarily elicit responses that tell you how likely someone is to perform well in a given environment.

For this reason, Enterprise has its recruiters focus on a technique that requires candidates to stay on their toes and demonstrate in a tangible way that they possess the core competencies the company is after. Enterprise realizes that bad hires can be very costly, making the up-front due diligence extremely important.

In behavioral interviews, you learn how people have acted in certain situations, which may be a good indication of how they'll perform if they come to work for you. After all, the most accurate predictor of future performance is what a person did in a similar situation in the past.

The core competencies for a management trainee and rental agent are very different, but both require the ability to deliver good customer service and solid communication skills. Behavioral interviewing can help assess whether someone has an ability to sell, for instance, much better than simply asking, "Do you enjoy sales?"

To gauge a candidate's sales ability, for instance, you might ask, "Tell me about a time when you had to persuade someone to buy into an idea or product." You can then follow up with questions like:

- What was the idea or product?
- What objections did you have to overcome?
- Were you successful?
- How did you measure success?

To assess a candidate's customer service skills you could ask the following:

- Can you tell me about a situation in which you had to resolve a customer complaint?
- How was it resolved?
- Did your manager have to take over?
- What did you learn from that experience?

Behavioral interview questions make it a lot easier to tell whether someone has had relevant experience, because if they can't quickly come up with a rational and believable scenario, they probably haven't lived it. Traditional questions make it much more likely that a candidate will tell you what he or she thinks you want to hear, rather than offering an honest assessment of his or her experiences.

I've also found that many candidates come to interviews prepared with answers to the standard questions they *think* you will ask. I remember one candidate who answered every question I threw his way without hesitation, and the answers all sounded wonderful. Trouble was, he didn't answer the questions I asked. I could tell he had rehearsed a series of responses based on what he thought I would ask, and he used them to address some completely unrelated queries. Needless to say, he didn't get the job.

Behavioral questions keep candidates on their toes. They're not easy to answer, but they paint a much clearer picture about someone's experience, providing a far better indication about how someone would likely act in a given role.

Some companies go beyond behavioral techniques by turning questions into brainteasers. At Google, for instance, don't be surprised if you're asked something like the following: "You are shrunk to the height of a nickel and thrown into a blender. Your mass is reduced so that your density is the same as usual. The blades start moving in sixty seconds. What do you do?" Land an interview at online shoe retailer Zappos and you might be asked, "On a scale of 1 to 10, how weird are you? Explain why you gave yourself that number." Apply for a position at Procter & Gamble and be prepared to answer this question: "How would you sell me an invisible pen?" And spirits maker Diageo is known to ask, "If you walk into a liquor store to count the unsold bottles but the clerk is screaming at you to leave, what do you do?"

Like most questions of this nature, there are no perfectly correct answers. Such queries are designed to see how a candidate thinks, determine whether he or she has the kind of experiences the company is after, measure intellect, and perhaps even provide a better glimpse into how someone might fit within the culture.

Similar behavioral questions should be thrown out to potential references supplied by job seekers, to figure out how well they really know the candidate. Harvard Business School is especially clever in this regard. It asks those who recommend a student to "describe the most important piece of constructive feedback you have given the applicant." If the reference can't answer this question, he or she probably doesn't know the candidate very well.

When analyzing candidates' responses to behavioral questions, Enterprise uses the STAR (Situation-Task-Action-Result) method. Simply put, look for the following elements:

- **Situation:** What situation or problem is the candidate describing?
- **Task:** What task was the candidate assigned to handle?
- **Action:** What action did the candidate take to resolve the situation or problem?
- **Result:** What was the outcome of the situation or problem?

Should a candidate fail to address all four elements, be sure to follow up and ask more probing questions until you get a complete response.

TAKE CANDIDATES ON A FIELD TRIP

Sometimes when you have a promising candidate but still aren't exactly sure from a standard interview alone whether he or she might fit well in your work environment, you might want to take things a step further by doing a field observation. Enterprise does this a lot with management trainees, so they can be very clear up front about what is expected of the role. A candidate is invited to a branch office and allowed to spend a short time (usually thirty to sixty minutes, though it could last longer in certain situations) watching others in the same position that he or she is applying for.

Observation lets a candidate see the conditions he or she would work under, the pace of the job, and the overall requirements. The candidate can ask questions in a less formal setting than the interview room and potentially meet the people he or she would be working with. It's also another chance to evaluate whether a candidate has the required core competencies. By the end of the observation, both sides should have a much better indication of whether the position is a good potential fit.

Observation also lets you know what a candidate is thinking based on the questions he or she asks. If Enterprise recruiters take someone out for a branch observation and the candidate ponders, "Do I really have to clean cars?" it provides an opportunity for the recruiter to probe further. Does the candidate not want to wash cars, or is he or she simply confirming that this is part of the job requirement? A candidate who expresses no hesitation about getting his or her hands dirty is demonstrating team spirit and a willingness to do what it takes to get the job done. If a candidate refuses to wash cars as part of the job, you know it's likely not going to work out for either side.

SAMPLE BEHAVIORAL QUESTIONS AND FOLLOW-UPS TO DETERMINE VARIOUS COMPETENCIES REQUIRED AT ENTERPRISE		
COMPETENCY	**QUESTION**	**FOLLOW-UP**
Dependability	Give me an example of when you had to go above and beyond to complete a task.	What was your role? What was the result? How successful were you?
Customer service (friendly, courteous attitude)	Tell me about a time when you were responsible for satisfying a customer.	What was the result? How successful were you? What kind of feedback did you get from your boss?
Attention to detail, thoroughness, cleanliness	If you were in this job, you would be required to clean cars and perform basic maintenance checks. Tell me about a time when you performed similar functions.	What did you like about the job? What did you find most challenging? What made you successful?
Ability to work under pressure in time-sensitive situations	Give me an example of when you had to meet a deadline that you hadn't anticipated. Provide an example of when you worked in a fast-paced environment.	What was the result? What did you like about working under those conditions? What was most frustrating about the situation? What kind of feedback did you get from your boss about the job you did?

WELCOME BACK BOOMERANGS

Despite its best efforts to drive loyalty, with a workforce of more than seventy thousand, it's not surprising that Enterprise loses a meaningful number of employees every year. Some decide working in the rental car business just isn't their cup of tea. Others leave to pursue what appears to be a better opportunity elsewhere. While many companies won't consider rehiring workers who leave, Enterprise often welcomes these so-called boomerang employees back.

Studies show that hiring former employees can save up to 50 percent on recruiting costs. In addition, boomerang hires tend to stay twice as long as workers recruited from the outside, and they are three times more likely to be top performers because they already understand the culture and expectations of the company.

Gary Palmer typifies the kind of boomerang hire that Enterprise often sees. Gary played basketball at California State University, Chico, and joined Enterprise after graduating in 1986. He began as a management trainee in Beverly Hills, California. Three months into the program, Palmer was recruited by his old college coach to play for the Dubbo Rams, a professional basketball team in Australia. Knowing that they allowed only two Americans onto the roster each year, he couldn't pass up this opportunity. "I traveled around South Wales, Australia, for the next two and a half years getting paid to play," Palmer says. "Even though I enjoyed the experience, I knew at the end of my second year that I wasn't going to make a living playing basketball."

Palmer thought about coming back to Enterprise upon returning to the United States, but back then rehiring former employees wasn't a widely accepted practice. Instead he took an industrial sales job with another company, but that lasted for less than a month. "I missed the people and the culture of Enterprise," he recalls, "not to mention the opportunity to run my own business."

He got in touch with some of his former colleagues, swallowed his pride, and asked them to let him come back. They did, and today Palmer is a general manager and director for Enterprise in the United Kingdom.

"As a fellow boomeranger, I've learned to keep in touch with those valued employees who leave for one reason or another," Palmer says. "As long as they know our doors are always open, we'll reinforce the fact that our company is a great place that is available for them to work."

If you have a good performer who decides to leave, keep in touch, since this person might just become your next best—and most loyal—hire some months or years down the line.

KEYS TO DRIVING LOYALTY BY ENGAGING YOUR WORKFORCE

1. Give workers a chance to share in the profits in order to instill a strong sense of engagement.
2. Promote from within to create a more stable work environment, encourage teamwork, and increase retention.
3. Allow employees the freedom to experiment and stretch themselves without fear of failure.
4. Create a culture with a set of values that you live and talk about all the time.
5. Provide employees with realistic goals about their growth potential in the organization over both the short term and the long haul.
6. Never commit to anything you won't be able to deliver on, since failing to keep your promises will cause you to lose all credibility.
7. Look for ways beyond money to motivate and instill loyalty.

8. Understand the motivating factors for those on your team, so you can structure appropriate incentive programs that encourage productivity and increase retention.
9. Use contests and competitions as a way to combine different motivating factors, such as winning, fun, accomplishment, and achieving goals.
10. Don't forget to recognize the runners-up as well, and use these experiences as opportunities to learn and grow.
11. Regularly praise and recognize high performers, to validate the work they are doing.
12. Create a fun atmosphere where people enjoy coming to work and are willing to do anything for you, your customers, and the company.
13. Match people up with mentors who are in the best position to help them grow.
14. Beyond standard benefits, use small gestures to impact loyalty, such as ordering in lunch on occasion or offering tickets to local shows.
15. Learn what matters most to your employees by asking them in an annual survey.
16. Find ways to support the charitable causes most important to those on your team.
17. Begin the engagement process before you hire by using behavioral interviewing techniques to identify those candidates most likely to fit best within your culture.

5 Lead with Empathy

Starbucks calls them partners. Walmart refers to them as associates. Disney brands them as cast members. Although various companies try to come up with clever names to refer to their workforce, Enterprise has found that how you treat employees is far more important than what you call them. And studies show that the number one driver of engagement is having a senior leader who inspires confidence.

"To be a good leader, you have to be able to read people and relate to them," says Matt Darrah, Enterprise's executive vice president of North American operations. "Good leaders are teachers. They have excellent social skills and realize that you have to communicate with people in different ways in order to make sure your message is not only heard but also acted upon. If you can't get through to people, it's very difficult to get results."

Above all, Enterprise believes that effective managers always lead with empathy.

"A good boss is someone who listens, who is open, and who is honest with you about how you're doing on the job," vice chairman Don Ross insists. "It's someone who has a true interest in you, not just in your career, but in you as a person."

When you think about it, most managers are focused exclusively on the task at hand. They spend their time making sure their teams get the job done and correct their course as necessary. But when was the last time you felt that your manager cared about you as a person? It turns out that this form of leadership actually improves on-the-job performance and can send engagement significantly higher.

"Part of my job in building employee loyalty is knowing about your goals, wants, and desires, and then helping you to achieve and fulfill them," says Enterprise chief strategy officer Greg Stubblefield.

"Loyalty comes from caring about your employees, their development, and their success," adds president and chief operating officer Pam Nicholson. "Whether you are leading to their strengths or supporting what they want to get out of their career, you want employees to believe that every decision you make is what's best not only for the company but also for their future. It's not about you. It's about them. And if they trust your decisions, they will follow your lead."

Earning this trust was a priority for Jack from the first day he started Enterprise. He realized that showing empathy was the best way to connect with his employees on a much higher level. So, in addition to talking with workers about their career ambitions, he also wanted to hear about their families and outside interests. In essence, he sought to understand what they valued most. It's a trait his son, Andy, has adopted as well.

"At some point in life as you move up in the organization you realize that you want to do everything you can to make the business and the people who work with you successful," Andy says. "It's about seeing great employees start early in their careers and grow into great team members, family members, community members, and businesspeople." Empathetic leaders take an interest in their employees and those things that are important to them. "I don't know the names of a lot of the children of our executives, especially now that our company is so big, but I generally know how many kids they have, and I see their spouses at least every couple of years, because that's a part of who these people are," Andy shares. "Jack's the same way. People sometimes get surprised when they see him and he asks about their kids by name. He always tries to relate to what he knows matters most to them."

In this chapter, we'll explore some of the ways that Enterprise works to drive loyalty by teaching its managers how to be empathetic—and therefore more effective—leaders. It largely has to do with thinking about people as individuals, not just as lines on an organizational chart. We'll also discuss what you can do to improve your skills in this area, allowing you to form a closer connection with the people you oversee.

THINK "WE," NOT "ME"

As an individual contributor, especially at a company such as Enterprise, you are always trying to get recognized and promoted. In order for this to happen, you have to set yourself apart from the rest of your colleagues. The way to do this is by showing initiative and drive, and proving you are worthy of promotion to the next level. But once you become a leader, you have to shift the focus from demonstrating what you can do to giving everyone under you the tools they need to succeed.

In other words, it's no longer about "me" but "we." A good leader helps others to do their very best and continually improve their performance. Effective leaders also serve as a role model for others to follow.

"People will do anything for a true leader because they possess qualities that go above and beyond just managing and executing," Nicholson insists. "A lot of people can execute yet have no loyalty. To be a good manager, it needs to be about more than all the things you are doing for yourself. It has to be about developing future leaders."

When leading a team it's important to remember that no one else will do things exactly the way you do. Your objective as a manager isn't to clone yourself. It's to help people develop their own skills and talents in order to be effective on the job. You are responsible for setting the vision, being an example, finding the best in your employees, and developing their skills.

Never try to push people to success. Instead, pull them toward it by getting buy-in and building on their strengths.

DOS AND DON'TS OF EMPATHETIC LEADERS	
LEADERS DO . . .	**LEADERS DON'T . . .**
Hold themselves accountable	Expect respect (they earn it)
Demonstrate excellent skills	Tell rather than ask
Achieve goals by leading and guiding others	Bark orders
Provide vision and direction	Jump in and do tasks for others
Praise people for team success	Blame others for team failures
Provide opportunities for others	Avoid less enjoyable assignments
Make themselves accessible and approachable	Command rather than guide
Stay positive, especially during tough times	Vent or complain to direct reports

UNDERSTAND THE LEADERSHIP MODEL

As a leader, you constantly have to balance two important and often conflicting goals: getting the job done and taking care of your people. How you do this is something your employees will watch, and your leadership style can affect them in ways you might not even be aware of.

The Enterprise leadership model provides a good guideline for gauging your management style and altering it to get the most out of your team. As you read through this section, figure out which style you fall into, and then determine what you might need to change in order to correct some of the perceptions your employees probably have about you.

Let's start at the bottom right quadrant with the Boss. This manager places a high priority on tasks and has less concern for people. Such a person tends to become authoritarian and has the opinion that "I'm the boss, so you should just do what I tell you." While employees who work for the Boss may be compliant, they likely won't remain very motivated.

ENTERPRISE LEADERSHIP MODEL

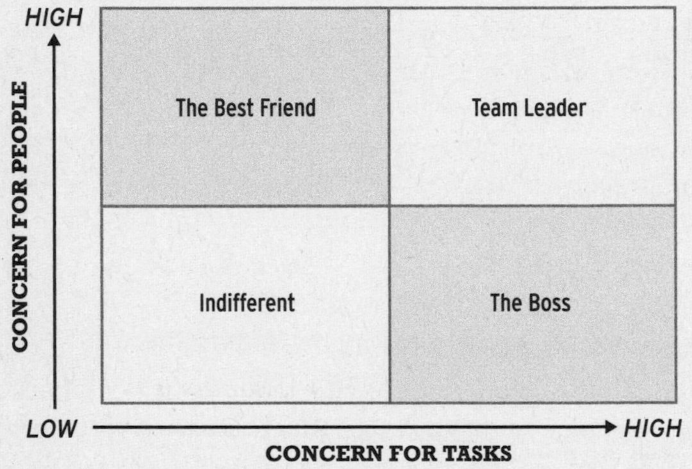

Next, moving clockwise, is the Indifferent style. It's rare to find a manager who has little concern for either tasks or people, but it's possible, especially if the manager is not engaged himself or herself. The Indifferent manager doesn't get much work done, and his or her team is therefore likely to be very unproductive.

The Best Friend is someone who has a high concern for people but is less focused on tasks. While on the surface you might think this would be the style most preferred by employees, but it's not. Such managers avoid holding employees accountable for fear of making them upset. Not only do employees not grow and learn, but they also are likely to take advantage of the manager before he or she ultimately loses any ability to lead.

Finally, the style that tends to be most effective is the Team

Leader. This person balances concern for both tasks and people. It can be the most challenging style to consistently maintain because of the competing demands on one's time and attention. To keep this balance, start by understanding the task at hand and then figure out how to address the empathetic or people side to get it done.

For instance, let's say you have an employee who consistently shows up late for work. You have previously addressed this issue but not seen any improvement. The employee is otherwise a strong worker and very capable at her job. After scheduling another feedback session to discuss the matter, you learn that the employee has a family member at home with health issues that require extra care in the morning. This is the reason she has arrived late for work so often.

To come up with a possible solution, it's helpful to first break this scenario down into both the task and the empathetic side. The task: help the employee to arrive at work on time. The empathetic side: help the employee deal with her family issue. One strategy for handling the matter is to be understanding and caring but let the employee know that tardiness is not acceptable. Express how much you value her, and let her know you're willing to work with her to find a mutually agreeable solution as long as it still meets the business need. You can start by asking the employee for ideas. In this case, if the business need allows, perhaps you can move her hours so she can start the day a bit later.

MANAGE ACCORDING TO THE EMPLOYEE LIFE CYCLE

Enterprise likes to think of the growing and nurturing of every worker according to what it calls the Employee Life Cycle. As demonstrated by the chart below, every time you hire or promote an employee, the cycle begins by setting goals and expectations. A goal is something like this: "Over the next ninety days, I expect you to become proficient at using our new software program." An expectation is something like this: "I expect every employee to provide outstanding service to our customers."

These goals and expectations should be reviewed and discussed on a regular basis, and more formally during the annual review.

The next step in the cycle is providing coaching and training, by equipping employees with the knowledge, tools, and skills they need to achieve the agreed-upon objectives. As a manager, you need to provide regular feedback to let employees know how you think they are doing. These efforts are designed to generate desired performance for the employee, helping them to advance in their job while at the same time achieving your business needs.

The cycle continually restarts with each promotion or delivery of new goals and expectations. In a moment we'll spend a bit more time discussing some of the key points on the cycle as they relate to providing feedback and coaching.

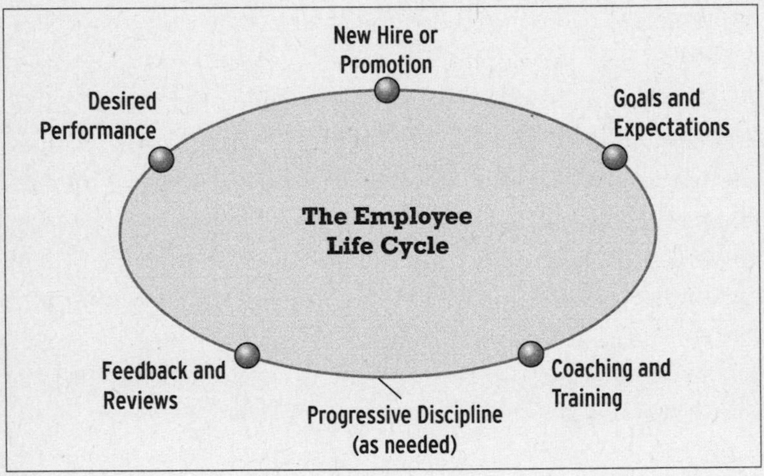

SEND OUT AN SOS

Once you have established specific goals, ongoing coaching is essential to developing your employees. Enterprise uses a coaching method known as SOS, which stands for "show, observe, and shape."

- **Show** employees how to perform a task while explaining the steps required to complete it.

- **Observe** employees as they perform the task.
- **Shape** performance by providing feedback, additional resources, or opportunities to improve their skills.

Coaching helps employees to better understand their strengths and weaknesses, while identifying steps they can take to get even better at what they do.

DELIVER CANDID FEEDBACK

Even though it may not always be positive, employees actually like to get feedback, and it should be delivered on a regular basis. "Effective leaders are good communicators," as Andy Taylor points out. One of the most important ways of communicating with your team is through periodic performance reviews.

Providing regular reviews helps to enhance both work output and morale by allowing employees to better understand their strengths and identify areas of improvement. This lets workers know where they stand and more clearly demonstrates where progress is being made. It's also an opportunity to set performance goals for the next review period, discuss opportunities for job growth and development, and recognize standout performance.

You should capture and present this feedback in writing at least once a year during the annual performance review. All managers are no doubt familiar with these documents, but the next time you have to prepare one, keep the following in mind:

- The review should be written *to*, not *about*, the employee.
- Focus on observable, job-related results and performance.
- Give an appropriate level of detail (not too general, yet not too specific).
- Provide tangible examples to support your ratings.
- Discuss accomplishments against goals established during the last review.

- Be sensitive in the words you use, avoiding generalities and the use of *always* and *never*.
- Don't offer any guarantees of employment or promotion.
- Never let recent negative behavior dominate the review.
- Be balanced, and don't come across as being either too lenient or overly critical.

Effective feedback focuses on specific behaviors, as opposed to vague generalities, attitudes, or personal characteristics. It reinforces actions that improve performance and redirects behavior that does not. It's also timed appropriately and stated respectfully.

For example, telling an employee, "You did a great job today. You're really amazing!" is nice, and will no doubt make the person feel good. But it doesn't tell the employee *why* he or she is amazing. A better approach is to explain the specific behavior that prompted your praise. Any feedback should be supported by a combination of follow-up conversations, documentation, and ongoing management to communicate clear expectations, establish a motivating work environment, and provide the proper training to help employees meet the requirements of the job.

Delivering feedback, especially when it's meant to redirect a behavior, can be difficult and even intimidating for some. Managers worry about offending employees or getting into an awkward dialogue that they may not be prepared to handle. To make the process easier, Enterprise uses a "state and wait" approach: state the behavior you want to redirect, then wait for the employee's response. Don't begin your comments by overemphasizing what's wrong with the behavior. Instead, simply state what the employee is doing and give the person a chance to respond. Chances are that he or she will recognize the problem right away and accept the need to change the behavior.

If the employee comes across as confused, resistant, or both, your challenge is to move past this confusion or resistance and toward acceptance. Along the way, you'll probably have to ask questions in order to better understand what your employees need from you to improve these behaviors.

Clarify expectations if the employee seems confused. If he or she resists your feedback by getting defensive or voicing objections, explain the impact the employee's behavior is having on others or on the business. Be prepared to offer tangible examples to back this up. If the employee accepts the need to change, you can provide coaching, an action plan, or both to help shape future performance.

HANDLING EMPLOYEE RESPONSES TO FEEDBACK

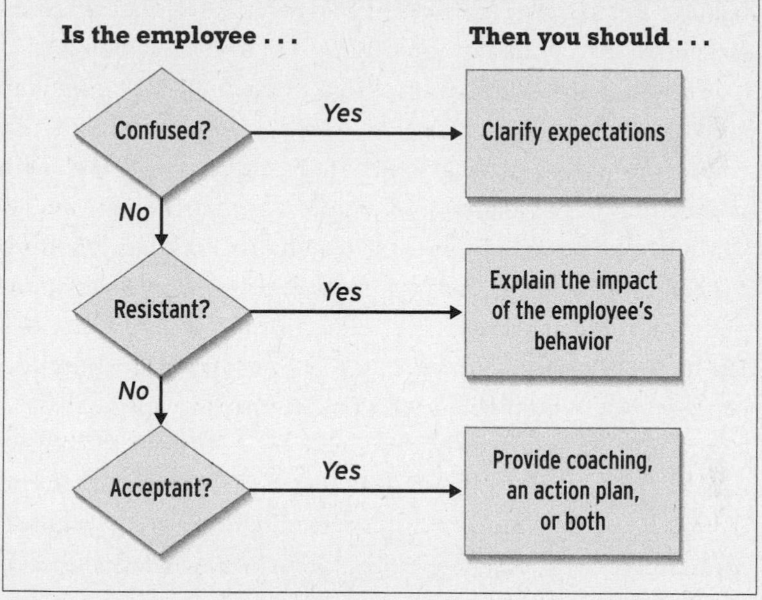

USE PROGRESSIVE DISCIPLINE

When coaching and feedback alone don't lead to improved performance, it may be necessary to move to progressive discipline. You'll notice it has a slight tail off the Employee Life Cycle, since it is not always required. Progressive discipline is used to improve performance and behaviors when feedback alone isn't effective. Its purpose is to convert undesirable behaviors into acceptable ones.

Progressive discipline is most successful when it helps

individuals become more effective performers. It is intended not to punish but rather to assist in improving deficiencies and satisfying job expectations.

Progressive discipline kicks in when attempts to improve performance through setting expectations, coaching, providing recognition, and feedback have failed. It is used when you want to retain an employee with the potential to be successful who is having challenges. Done right, progressive discipline shows an employee that the manager cares and wants him or her to succeed. Nevertheless, if an employee still fails to bring performance to an acceptable level after being given numerous opportunities, progressive discipline can sometimes lead to termination.

There are three steps to progressive discipline. It starts with a *verbal warning*, in which you have a conversation with the employee about the behavior in need of improvement. This should take place as soon as possible after the occurrence and be carefully documented in writing. Second is a *written notice from the manager*, detailing the performance issue, expectations, and potential further consequences. The third step, if the first two fail to yield results, is *having a heart-to-heart about whether that person should still stay with your company*. It just may be that a separation is best for both sides.

Most employees can be influenced to perform better. In any company about 10 percent of your team will consist of star performers, while another 10 percent will cause challenges, regardless of how they are managed. The 80 percent in the middle can go either way and tend to benefit most from coaching and progressive discipline.

"Effective discipline always revolves around honesty," Darrah explains. "If I'm not honest about how you're doing, I'm not doing me, you, or the team any good. I'm not talking about being honest at the end of the road and saying, 'You're not good at this, so we're letting you go.' By then it's too late. I'm talking about being honest along the way, telling you how you might want to course-correct. If I don't see progress, it becomes a much more frank discussion about how I've given you all these tools but you've chosen not to use them. At this point we're in the progressive discipline stage. But the bottom line is you can't manage or discipline everyone the exact same way. It won't work. You need to read every employee and do your best to figure out which form of discipline is likely to be most effective for that individual."

Progressive Discipline Checklist

Apply progressive discipline when you see no positive changes and have already done the following:

- ☑ Clearly communicated expectations
- ☑ Given any necessary coaching (including specific feedback), training, and practice
- ☑ Offered appropriate rewards (i.e., praise and recognition) for good performance
- ☑ Provided the tools and processes the employee needs to perform to your expectations

DELEGATE RESPONSIBILITY

It's very easy, especially when you're a high performer, to simply want to do the job yourself, particularly when an employee you manage is not handling it as well as you could on your own. But the ability to delegate is an important aspect of being an empathetic leader. Delegation enables the people under you to develop new skills under your guidance and coaching. It also frees you up from tasks that can be effectively performed by someone else.

Delegation benefits you, the employee, and your entire team. It gives you more time to deal with strategy and planning, and it allows you to feel less pressure. Delegation also empowers your employees to be more confident and increases their skills, while helping you and your team achieve results in less time. And it gives employees a sense of responsibility and a chance to grow, learn, and contribute.

There are two primary reasons to delegate tasks: to improve results and to develop employees. Once you have established goals for your team, the only way to complete them is by delegating many of the tasks to others. At the same time, delegation allows employees to expand their own skills and feel that they are part of a successful team. The best leaders are those who help employees to grow and to achieve results. It's not about working the most hours, and there is no need to believe you have to perform every task by yourself because others aren't as capable.

Keep in mind that this isn't about delegating only those responsibilities you don't want to handle yourself. It's about letting everyone be a part of achieving the goals you have set for the business.

To effectively delegate a task you need to first share the big picture. Explain why the responsibility is being delegated and be clear about its relevance and importance. Describe the task to be accomplished and get clarifying feedback to make sure the employee understands what needs to be done. Next, come to agreement on resources, priorities, and deadlines. Finally, make sure the employee understands how you will judge whether the job has been performed to your satisfaction. After the task is completed, it's crucial to follow up and monitor the employee's progress, providing candid feedback along the way.

HAVE A PLAN

Good leaders always have a plan in place so that they know what needs to be accomplished and can delegate appropriately. Planning ahead ensures that all the tasks will be taken care of, creates a smoother flow to the day, reduces stress, and impacts both employee and customer satisfaction. Planning means knowing *what* needs to be done, prioritizing *when* to do it, and deciding *who* should complete the task.

When you don't plan, you will find yourself constantly reacting to situations you aren't prepared to deal with. In addition, employee performance will drop because development gets neglected and important tasks won't get done. Leaders who plan ahead exude confidence and control, keeping everyone calm and providing a model for others to follow.

SET S.M.A.R.T. GOALS

What do we mean by S.M.A.R.T. goals?

- **S = Stretch.** The goal must represent a stretch—a challenging but attainable improvement over your current level of achievement.
- **M = Measurable.** You must be able to measure whether the goal is being achieved, using a tool that is clear, concise, and easy to use.
- **A = Action-oriented.** The goal must state in clear terms the action or result you want to achieve.
- **R = Realistic.** The goal must be realistic and achievable based on your previous experiences.
- **T = Time-based.** The goal must state a time frame for completion.

S.M.A.R.T. goals should include both personal and team goals. Make sure that employees are involved in the goal-setting process and buy into what you have set out for them to achieve. If they aren't committed, the goals won't be realized.

FOSTER OPEN COMMUNICATION

Following the acquisition of Alamo and National, employees at all three Enterprise brands had lots of questions: Would they still have a job? What impact would the sale have on compensation and benefits?

At all times, but especially in periods of change, good leaders communicate regularly with their teams in an open and honest way.

"During the transition period, we got out there right away as a management team and essentially said, 'We're going to get through this together,'" Stubblefield shares. "We told them that whether they came through the farm system at Enterprise or were an acquired free agent through the transaction, they were still on the team. But we were also quick to say we hadn't figured everything out yet and it would take some time for us to do this."

Leaders were honest enough to let some employees know that they probably weren't the best fit for the Enterprise culture. "Those were some difficult discussions, but it's really in the spirit of doing what's best for both the company and the employee," Stubblefield adds. "Making tough decisions like that is part of what it means to be a leader."

You may wonder whether it's possible to mix having to terminate someone with being empathetic. The truth is, you'll generally find that when things get to the point where you have to let someone go, quite often the decision to terminate is best for both sides. Employees generally can tell when they're not doing well, and likely it's because of apathy that they haven't decided to leave on their own. By being transparent, straightforward, and factual, in most cases you'll earn the respect of the employee, who will recognize that in the long run you are actually doing him or her a favor.

FOLLOW THE GOLDEN RULE

At the end of the day, an empathetic leader treats everyone exactly as he or she wants to be treated. When you take the time to understand what employees value and where they want to go in their careers, they will be honest with you and you will quickly earn their loyalty. Leading with empathy inspires creative thinking, creates mutual trust, and helps you to better understand what other people may be thinking or feeling. It also significantly increases the likelihood that everyone on your team will stay motivated and willing to do whatever it takes to make you and the entire business succeed.

KEYS TO DRIVING LOYALTY BY LEADING WITH EMPATHY

1. Listen, be open, and provide employees with honest feedback about how they are performing on the job.
2. To better connect with the members of your team, seek to understand what they value most, and let them know you care about them.
3. Shift the focus from "me" to "we" and serve as a role model for others to follow.
4. Instead of trying to clone yourself, help those you manage to develop their own skills and talents.
5. Be a team leader by learning to balance your concerns for both tasks and people.
6. Seek to grow and nurture everyone on your team according to the Employee Life Cycle.
7. Coach your employees by using the SOS method: show, observe, and shape.
8. Communicate regularly, and provide both written and verbal feedback on a regular basis, focusing on observable, job-related results and performance.
9. When delivering feedback, state the behavior you want to redirect, then wait for the employee's response.
10. Use progressive discipline when necessary to help those you want to retain become more effective performers.
11. Always have a plan in place so that you know what needs to be accomplished and can delegate appropriately.
12. Treat everyone you manage exactly as you would want to be treated yourself in order to inspire creative thinking and an attitude of being willing to do whatever it takes to make the business succeed.

6 Deliver Dazzling Service

Although Enterprise has endeavored to deliver excellent customer service since the day Jack Taylor opened his doors in 1957, the company didn't start to formally monitor how well it was doing in this area until 1989. That's when Enterprise Rent-A-Car commissioned its first national television commercial. The spot featured an Enterprise employee handing over the keys to what the announcer referred to as the customer's "own car," capitalizing on the personalized pickup service the company had become known for.

As is typical in the ad industry, follow-up research was conducted with a handful of customers who rented from Enterprise to gather their impressions about both the commercial and their actual experience in dealing with the company. While the ad won high praise, not all customers were happy with Enterprise. Some complained about getting dirty cars, a few didn't get picked up on time, and others seemed generally dissatisfied with the overall treatment. The feedback wasn't scientific by any means, but it raised some serious concerns at Enterprise headquarters.

Perplexed, Andy Taylor ordered some additional surveys. He wanted more intelligence to better understand how well the company was delivering on its mission to exceed customer expectations. As mixed results continued to flow in, Andy realized more needed to be done, and quickly.

"By 1994, we were growing very fast and had more than four thousand locations," Andy recalls. "Revenues had jumped from $200 million to around $2 billion over the previous ten years, and we were opening a branch a day. Despite this success, I was starting to get calls, letters, and other feedback suggesting that the consistency of our service was falling short of where we expected it to be. It validated some of the responses we heard in these focus groups."

MEASURE, THEN MANAGE

Back then there wasn't a lot of research into the field of customer satisfaction, since it was a relatively new area of study. Enterprise decided to assemble an internal team to create an official customer survey. They set out to learn more about how customers felt, at least at a high level, but kept coming up with new things to ask: "Were you treated as though you were a valued customer? How satisfied were you with the Enterprise employees you dealt with? With their courtesy? Their professionalism? Their promptness? The selection of cars? The mechanical condition of the vehicle? The car's cleanliness inside and out? The overall price? The time it took to complete the transaction? The pickup service?" Before long, the survey grew to eighteen questions, ending with a request for customers to grade their Enterprise experience on a five-point scale ranging from completely satisfied (5) to completely dissatisfied (1).

The first survey was mailed out to sixteen hundred customers in July 1994. It was based on a random sampling of renters around the country and was designed to go out quarterly. Response rates were around 25 percent, considerably lower than Enterprise initially anticipated. The team ultimately realized that the survey had too many questions. Just looking at the list was overwhelming. Plus, since the survey arrived by mail, it was easy for people to simply throw it away unless they had a compelling reason to send it back.

ENTERPRISE'S SPECTRUM OF CUSTOMER SATISFACTION

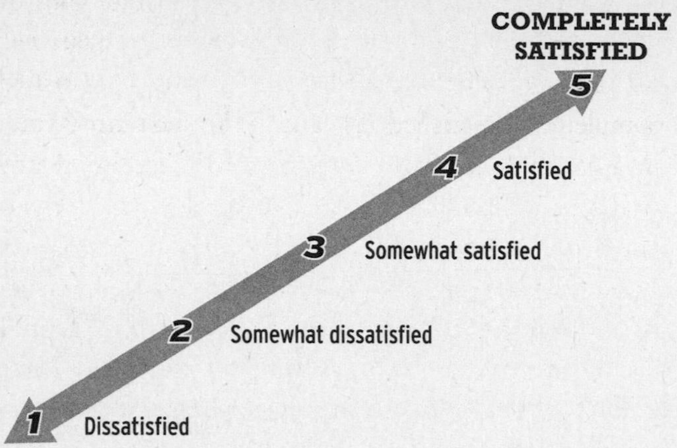

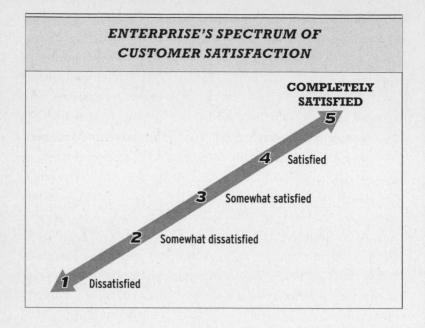

The surveys that did get returned revealed that customer service wasn't top-of-mind for all Enterprise branches. Many customers were downright unhappy, and overall scores were much lower than anyone had thought. What made this surprising to many Enterprise executives was that revenues were at an all-time high. This caused a number of managers to question the validity of the responses. They rationalized that if things were really as bad as the results suggested, business wouldn't be so good. There was also no proof at this point that boosting customer satisfaction would increase profitability.

"To be perfectly honest, before we started the survey, we measured customer service based on how fast our business was expanding," admits Enterprise vice chairman Don Ross. "We went on gut feelings but had no tangible evidence."

Enterprise realized that continuing to conduct regular surveys was essential. However, given these early experiences, the company made four significant changes to its approach. First, it hired an outside firm to ask the questions. Second, it began to conduct the survey by phone, calling customers just a day or two after completing their rental, when the experience was still fresh in their mind. This gave Enterprise more immediate feedback and significantly boosted response rates from 25 percent to 98 percent. Third, the company dropped the number of questions down to just two: "How would you rate your overall experience?" using a five-point scale of completely satisfied (5), satisfied (4), somewhat satisfied (3), somewhat dissatisfied (2), and completely dissatisfied (1), and "The next time you need to rent a car, how likely are you to call Enterprise, Alamo, or National again?" using a similar five-point scale. If customers gave the company a 1 or a 2, especially on the second question, the survey taker apologized for the disappointing experience and asked for permission to have a branch manager follow up. In 95 percent of the cases, customers were open to having this communication. The whole process of getting through the survey took less than sixty seconds.

Strategies for Conducting Effective Customer Surveys

1. Use an outside company whenever possible.
2. Conduct surveys in person or by phone.
3. Keep the number of questions to a minimum (usually no more than three).
4. Give people a satisfaction scale of 1 to 5.
5. Conclude with an open-ended question for general feedback.
6. Follow up with anyone who expresses anything but complete satisfaction.

The final change was that surveys were taken and the results tracked at an individual branch level. This was something a number of managers initially resisted. For starters, they were going to be charged for the cost of the survey. Because bonuses are based largely on branch profitability, managers don't like to spend money unnecessarily. More important, the skeptics felt that they already knew how they were doing based on feedback they personally solicited from customers at each branch.

To appease their concerns, Ross proposed a compromise. "We asked everyone to predict what score they would get if we sent a survey to their customers," Ross shares. "We then went out to those customers and compared the results." What they found is that managers had about a 50 percent rate of accuracy in determining their scores—not much better than a random guess. This convinced just about everyone that without some kind of tangible outside research it was nearly impossible to determine how customers really felt. Furthermore, they found that the lowest-performing branches, in terms of profitability, had the lowest customer service scores, helping to validate the notion that happy customers lead to a more robust bottom line.

As a result of its survey work, Enterprise Rent-A-Car built a system known as ESQi, which stands for the Enterprise Service Quality Index. Every Enterprise branch is assigned its own ESQi score, which represents the percentage of customers who report being completely satisfied with their rental experience. Enterprise sends over contact information for every customer at the completion of each rental to the outside research firm, which then calls a random sampling of customers with a goal of completing twenty-five surveys for each branch every month. That amounts to about two hundred thousand people, or 5 percent of the four million customers the company serves, who get called on a monthly basis. If, during the course of the conversation, the survey taker realizes a customer is not happy, he or she sends a message to the branch manager and area general manager to follow up.

The scores are then averaged to come up with an overall company number. ESQi results are continually measured and reported weekly, although they are considered to be statistically valid only when viewed on a monthly and quarterly basis. The scores are completely transparent across the company. Every branch, area, and group knows everyone else's ESQi score.

ESQi has since served as the inspiration behind other similar programs, including the Net Promoter Score developed by Fred Reichheld of Bain & Company.

Alamo and National didn't do surveys in this manner until Enterprise took over both companies. They did, however, conduct what are known as Brand Integrity Audits. In essence, an assessor was sent to each location to walk through the rental process, evaluating everything from the level of customer service to vehicle cleanliness, shuttle bus service, brand image, facilities, wait time, and so forth. The assessor looked at those elements that matter most to customers from the moment they step on the airport shuttle to when they return their car at the end. Enterprise decided to marry the two approaches after the acquisition. It began to survey Alamo and National customers by phone, while implementing the Brand Integrity Audit at all Enterprise airport locations.

"Assessors travel every day of the week and spend time making sure our processes are consistent across every location in accordance with the standards we have set for each brand," explains Rob Hibbard, Enterprise's vice president for airport operations. The company views the surveys and audits as being the science behind how to deliver first-rate service.

"The secret to building customer loyalty is having that consistency from location to location," adds chief strategy officer Greg Stubblefield. "You want people to have the same experience with your company on every visit and in every city. That's what helps to build loyalty. It's not just a fluke that you had a good experience. It's something that gets repeated over and over, reinforcing your commitment to your customers."

This concept of consistency is essential regardless of your business. If you run a restaurant chain, for example, customers expect your food to taste the same at every location they visit. Hotel chains must also work hard to instill a consistent brand experience in all parts of the world so that travelers know what kind of accommodations and service to expect. If a customer has just one bad experience at any location in the system—even if it was a one-off situation—that person might never do business with the company again.

A few final words about surveys. While every business should use them to some degree, approach customers for feedback very carefully and don't overwhelm their time. Asking someone to take a few minutes to share their thoughts once a year is fine, but going after customers following each transaction can lead to survey fatigue. Thanks to cheap technology that allows online surveys to be conducted for free, many companies send emails asking to be rated after every transaction. This gets annoying and has led to an overall decline in survey response rates over the last ten years. Some retailers and restaurants implore customers to provide feedback on every sale at the bottom of their receipts, sometimes offering a chance to win a small prize or get a free appetizer on the next visit for doing so. This type of impersonal survey work sends a message that you don't really care but are just checking off the boxes by asking everyone for feedback. A more personalized and infrequent approach is bound to elicit a higher response rate and more thoughtful interaction, since customers will feel as if you personally selected them to participate and are really concerned about what they have to say.

GO BEYOND SATISFACTION

Even before ESQi was a thought in anyone's mind, Jack kept telling employees, "Repeat customers are the quickest way to build a solid business." Having people come back again and again is the essence of customer loyalty. The way you earn this loyalty, Jack maintained, was by wowing every person who walks in your door. The more managers began to analyze ESQi scores, the more they realized he was exactly right.

A lot of companies lump "completely satisfied," "satisfied," and "somewhat satisfied" into the same boat and figure that if they hit any of these marks, they're doing well. But Enterprise found there was a huge gap between the two categories. Nearly 75 percent of those in the "completely satisfied" category reported that they would definitely use Enterprise again the next time they rented a car. Only 29 percent of "somewhat satisfied" customers vowed to return. The company then compared these intentions to actual behavior and found that "top-box" customers—those who gave the company a score of 5—were, in fact, generating repeat business. Those with a rating of 4, or satisfied, were far less likely to do the same. "This proved that customer satisfaction wasn't just a soft management issue," Andy Taylor concluded. "It has a direct impact on the bottom line." It was also in sync with research showing that a customer's loyalty to a brand increases only a minimal amount between the "completely dissatisfied" and "somewhat satisfied" ratings. Loyalty takes a dramatic jump only for those in the "completely satisfied" category.

"COMPLETELY SATISFIED" CUSTOMERS ARE MUCH MORE LIKELY TO RETURN THAN THE MERELY "SATISFIED"

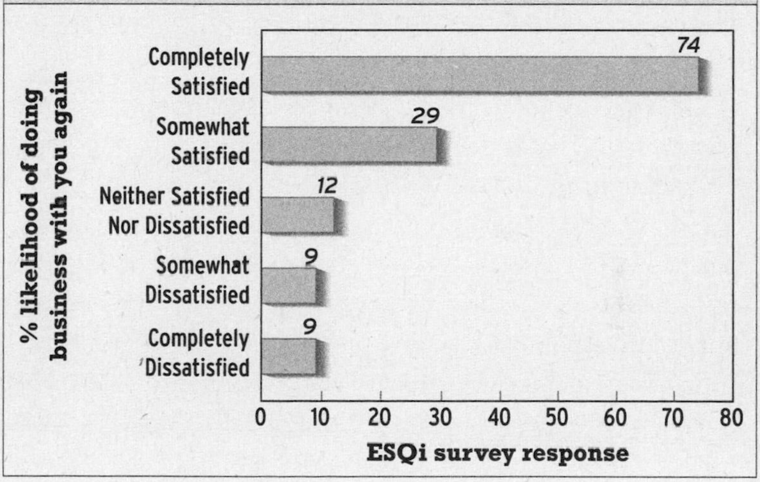

HOLD EMPLOYEES ACCOUNTABLE

As helpful as the ESQi numbers were, initially Enterprise didn't hold people accountable for earning high scores. That changed in October 1996. At the company's annual meeting for senior managers in Turnberry Isle, Florida, there was a lot to celebrate. Enterprise Rent-A-Car had just become the largest rental car company in the United States, surpassing Hertz, and profits were at an all-time high. The company had also refined its ESQi process and was about to reveal the latest survey results before the crowd gathered in the grand ballroom. Jack Taylor was seated in the back and eagerly awaited the results. But as the numbers were revealed, an audible gasp of disappointment could be heard. Scores were below projected targets across the board, and there was a big gap between the best- and worst-performing branches. Even more troubling, insurance adjusters, which represented a key customer group, rated Enterprise below a prime competitor. Jack was visibly upset, and went over to see Andy during the break.

"Andrew," he said, "we've got a big problem."

That grabbed Andy's attention. His father hadn't called him Andrew in about thirty years. "While Enterprise had grown far beyond his dreams, Jack worried the company was in danger of losing touch with the core values that formed the foundation of its success," Andy says.

Later that evening, Jack called the ESQi results "a slap in the face" and challenged company leaders to turn the disappointing numbers around. A decision was immediately made to make ESQi the foremost measure by which the company was managed. They also decided to start holding every employee accountable for exceeding customer expectations, and therefore for delivering high ESQi scores.

From that point on, in order for you to be promoted, your branch had to generate an above-average ESQi score. This way, it directly impacted everyone's pocketbook and created a huge financial incentive, because the way managers earn a higher bonus is by getting promoted.

"We make a big deal out of ESQi numbers," Andy Taylor says. "We post the scores prominently in our monthly operating reports right next to the profit numbers that determine managers' pay. Operating managers can see how well they and their peers are doing because everyone gets ranked from top to bottom."

Any doubts about how serious Enterprise was about its commitment to tie scores to compensation were put to rest when a prominent group vice president who always posted outstanding financial results was passed over for a promotion because of his group's low ESQi scores. "We found out he was keeping his expenses low by not having enough employees, and the workers he had were getting burned out," Andy says. "At the same time, the counter sales process was not especially customer friendly. He was making a lot of money but wasn't getting good customer satisfaction ratings. Our refusal to promote him sent a clear message that we took ESQi very seriously."

There are now four SQi scores across the organization: ASQi (Alamo Service Quality Index), NSQi (National Service Quality Index), ESQi (Enterprise Service Quality Index), and TSQi (Taylor Service Quality Index, which measures the average score across all three brands).

While Alamo and National both valued the importance of customer service before being taken over by Enterprise, employees of the brands hadn't been formally trained in the art of how to deliver it. Enterprise began to teach the skills it had passed on to its own team during the previous five decades, and got these new employees to quickly embrace its customer-centered culture. About a year after the acquisition, the company took a test measure of SQi scores for Alamo and National and found that the Enterprise formula for delivering a great customer experience worked well across these other brands, too. On the first go-round, Alamo got a 74 and National came in at 77 (on a scale of 1 to 100). These scores didn't yet count in terms of impacting employee compensation, but soon afterward, the company started to tie bonuses for hourly employees at Alamo and National into their branch SQi scores. During subsequent periods, the ASQi and NSQi scores moved higher: Alamo's rose to 78 and National's to 82, moving ahead of Enterprise's at 80.

What does Enterprise know about delivering great customer service that you can implement in your own business? Throughout the rest of this chapter we'll explore what the company teaches its employees about how some of the small things can make a huge difference in driving customer loyalty for your business.

GO BEYOND THE BASICS

When Enterprise executives first started to think about the elements of customer satisfaction, they assumed that things such as having a clean, well-maintained car were at the top of the list. They couldn't have been more wrong. Sure, that helped, since giving customers a dirty vehicle is bound to make them unhappy. But those are basic expectations people have of every car rental company. It's no different from ordering a cheeseburger at McDonald's. You don't get any more excited after finding it has cheese. That's your minimum expectation. You'll be angry if the cheese isn't there, but you won't give the restaurant extra points for handing you a hot hamburger complete with all the ingredients you ordered.

What will really make your company stand out is working with your employees to create a welcoming experience where customers feel special and well treated. While the general components of excellent customer service are the same for everyone, different aspects may mean more to one customer than to another. By the same token, knowing what customers expect is also important. For instance, first-class travelers on Virgin Atlantic's flights from the United States to London want far more than just a safe journey across the pond. They want to get there in style and arrive relaxed. For many this means the ability to get plenty of uninterrupted sleep so they can arrive fresh and ready to go. To that end, after talking to customers, Virgin realized that having peace and quiet during the flight was extremely important. So, beyond providing good service, the airline hired a "whispering coach" to teach flight attendants how to speak in a low tone once the lights were dimmed in the airline's Upper Class Dream Suites. In addition to learning to whisper at 20 to 30 decibels (compared to the normal speaking volume of 60 to 70 decibels), flight attendants are trained to read passengers in order to determine what level of service they expect. They are also instructed how to properly wake them from a deep sleep. The airline even built a buffer into the cabin so that passengers aren't bothered by the noisy snores of their seatmates.

Behaviors That Move Customer Service from Good to Excellent

- Smiling—even when customers can't see you
- Acknowledging each customer warmly and promptly
- Making eye contact
- Shaking a customer's hand
- Saying "please" and "thank you"
- Using the customer's name
- Talking with an interested, enthusiastic tone of voice
- Maintaining a positive attitude
- Being polite and sincere
- Having a sparkle in your eyes
- Exceeding expectations by doing more than the customer asks

ACKNOWLEDGE CUSTOMERS BY NAME

Have you ever walked into a store with a long line and felt frustrated because the employees at the counter were moving at a snail's pace, seemingly oblivious to the fact that there was a bunch of anxious people waiting to be served? In such situations, your inclination is no doubt to march out the door and into the arms of a more welcoming competitor. But let's assume that instead the clerk looks up as you walk in, thanks you for coming, apologizes for the wait, and assures you that he or she will get to you as soon as possible. All of a sudden your patience gets extended, you feel important, and you're more willing to wait a few extra minutes, despite still being in a hurry.

Enterprise teaches employees to always look up and make eye contact with anyone who comes into a branch office. A simple hello and acknowledgment can do wonders. Even better is to recognize customers by name, especially if it's someone who comes in frequently. There's nothing more magical to someone than the sound of his or her own name. One coffee shop I frequent has mastered this technique. Even though I stop by only twice a week, when I come in someone on the staff always looks up and says, "Hi, Kirk. Good to see you today." What's more, they all remember what drink I always order (a large dry decaf iced Americano) and start to make it the moment I walk in. So even when there's a line, by the time I get to the front my drink is usually waiting for me. Although there are plenty of other coffee shops nearby, some of which are cheaper, I'm extremely loyal to this particular location because of the way I'm treated. I feel a connection to the employees and wouldn't consider going anywhere else. I actually look forward to seeing the entire staff, and know all of their names as well. That's exactly the kind of loyalty and commitment you should strive to earn from your customers.

PROVIDE THE RIGHT LEVEL OF SERVICE

Ironically, sometimes less is more when it comes to providing personalized service. Good waiters are taught to read their customers as soon as they arrive at the table. If diners appear to be in a hurry, a good waiter will focus on getting the order taken and food delivered fast, rather than trying to be chatty and attempting to create a memorable and relaxing evening. If instead the diners appear to be out for a romantic evening, a good waiter will spend a lot of time up front introducing himself or herself, discussing some of the specials for the evening, making recommendations, and encouraging the patrons to take their time. Both approaches can ultimately lead to delighted customers—and generate a nice tip—since they equally meet the patrons' expectations. For the table in a hurry, getting them out faster than they expected is what will delight them. Try to rush the couple on a date and you'll be criticized for not creating a relaxing environment. It's all about knowing what the customer wants. Those in the restaurant business refer to this as "having eyes for" or "reading" your table. Chains such as T.G.I. Friday's and Romano's Macaroni Grill have realized the importance of this and now regularly train service staff to make note of body language and offhand remarks. For instance, when a waiter returns a few minutes after delivering the order to ask, "How is everything?" if a patron responds, "Oh, it's okay" or if someone in the group comments, "I've had better," the waiter knows the customers are unhappy and is supposed to proactively try to remedy the situation. The waiter's tip and the restaurant's reputation depend on it.

The same thing applies to the car rental industry. While delivering top-notch personalized service is appropriate most of the time, on occasion renters just want to get in and out as quickly as possible, sometimes without even talking to a human being. That's especially true with National customers, who tend to be business executives on a tight schedule. In Chapter 7 we'll discuss how the brand has employed technology in effective ways to create a seamless—and fast—customer experience.

ALWAYS ASK THREE CRITICAL QUESTIONS

To get a sense of how customers feel, look for verbal cues. Enterprise employees across all three brands are trained to ask customers three things before closing out each rental transaction:

- How was our service?
- What could we have done to make your experience better?
- If there was a misstep, what can we do to make it up to you?

Every employee is empowered to act upon that last question, and each branch has what is known as a customer accommodation account. This is used to fund actions needed to resolve situations where the company has fallen short. Often the resolution involves some sort of credit on the customer's bill. In such cases, agents will clearly show the reduction as a line item credit on the customer's final invoice, as a visual reminder of the company's good faith gesture. Customer accommodation accounts work both ways. If a branch spends too little in this area, it raises a red flag that employees might not be doing enough. But if the costs are unusually high, it signals that there could be a persistent problem in need of attention.

Customer responses to all three critical questions get logged and tracked in what's known as a Success/Failure Log. Enterprise encourages employees to write down customer comments in the log as they speak, to show that customers' opinions are important and are being recorded. Noting this feedback in the log helps to identify trends that may enhance or hinder complete satisfaction. "We're constantly looking for ways to understand what's going on in our customers' minds," says Dan Gass, Enterprise's vice president of customer experience. "The branches that perform best eat, live, and breathe customer service. There's not a conversation that goes by without asking, 'How are our customers doing today?' " The best lessons from these experiences are discussed during internal meetings referred to as the Vote, where coworkers share constructive feedback, honor an employee who has demonstrated the best customer service skills, and recognize people who have significantly improved their customer service skills since the previous meeting.

It's essential to address any issues immediately. A recent study from Arizona State University shows that only 21 percent of people who complain are satisfied with the ultimate resolution. If a customer is unhappy, your best chance of turning the situation around is while the problem is fresh, and before the customer has to file an official complaint. If you let someone leave your place of business angry, the frustration will only start to build. He or she will probably start to spread negative information about your company to friends and family. With social media so prevalent today, chances are an unhappy customer may even go online and start blogging about his or her experiences or posting comments on various review sites. By the time the customer actually gets around to complaining to someone higher up in the company, he or she will be *really* angry. Failing to respond to these complaints right away will likely result in losing the customer forever.

"We want every customer to walk away with the same sense that Jack Taylor instilled at the very beginning, and that means having people say, 'This is a great place to do business,'" Gass adds. Keep in mind that, above all, angry customers want to feel as if they are being heard, so it's crucial to always respond by acknowledging the problem, showing you understand the situation, and promising to do what you can to make things right. That will create a bond with the customer, especially if he or she senses you are truly committed to resolving the situation.

Three Steps to Dealing with Negative Customer Feedback

1. Assess the situation.
    - Ask open-ended questions.
    - Allow the customer to explain what happened.

2. Assess the customer.
    - Determine the level of the customer's dissatisfaction.
    - Figure out what it will take to satisfy the customer.

3. Take action.
    - Apologize.
    - Resolve the issue.

One primary objective of measuring ESQi was for Enterprise to understand those areas where it was falling short. But the company discovered that Alamo and National were keeping track of customer *compliments* as well.

"At first, we kind of thought that was a little silly," Gass admits. "We figured there wasn't a lot to learn from all the things people said you were doing right. But in reality this was a brilliant idea. When you recognize your employees for great work, it gets them excited and enthusiastic about continuing to wow the next customer who comes in." Not surprisingly, the practice was adopted throughout the entire organization.

Reasons Customers Don't Complain

1. They fear it won't do any good.
2. They think complaining is difficult.
3. They feel awkward about saying anything negative.
4. There are plenty of competitors, so it's easy for them to just take their business elsewhere.

CAPITALIZE ON THE CYCLE OF SERVICE

Every interaction with customers consists of a series of moments of truth. Each moment represents a specific opportunity that you have to make an impression. To better illustrate this, let's explore the Cycle of Service for Enterprise Rent-A-Car, which consists of eight identifiable moments during the rental process. Many of these elements now also apply to National and Alamo, except for those services unique to Enterprise, such as the pickup and dealing with insurance claims. If each moment, or personal interaction, is handled effectively, it should ultimately lead to complete customer satisfaction.

THE ENTERPRISE CYCLE OF SERVICE

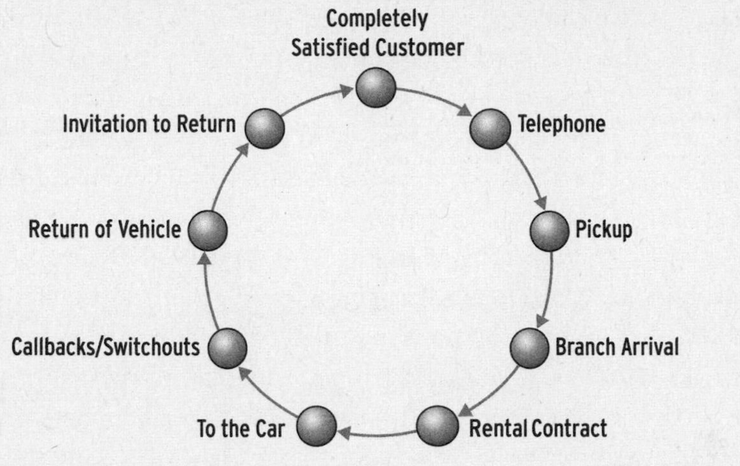

Telephone

The first moment of truth is generally a telephone call by the customer to an Enterprise branch requesting a car. Or, if the reservation was made online, it may be someone phoning in for directions or to confirm some detail about the rental. Since the interaction is not in person, what the employee says is vital.

It's important to smile while talking to customers on the phone, because they really can hear this in your voice. If you don't believe that, try saying the following sentence in a monotone with a straight face: "We really look forward to seeing you later today and will do everything we can to make your experience with us as enjoyable as possible."

Now read that same sentence again, but with a smile on your face.

Notice a difference?

During the call, it's also crucial to use the customer's name, and remember it's the first of many opportunities to thank the customer for his or her business.

In addition, employees avoid putting callers on hold whenever possible. A huge pet peeve of mine is calling a business and getting a recorded message telling me that all lines are busy, especially when the message is delivered in a tone that sounds completely insincere, right up to the "We apologize for any inconvenience and appreciate your patience." Worse yet, I've called some businesses and gotten a recording saying that all lines are busy and telling me to call back later. Talk about frustrating! If you have an automated hold attendant at your business, configure it to give customers options. For instance, during busy periods, the automated attendant at Southwest Airlines lets customers enter a phone number and have an agent automatically call them back as soon as one is available. This saves callers from having to stay on hold listening to stale music, yet prevents them from losing their place in the queue. Ideally, you should answer the phone in person and ask permission to place a caller on hold. In such cases, don't press the hold button until the caller gives you an answer. I've phoned many businesses where someone says, "Can you please hold?" and then proceeds to put me on hold before I can even utter a yes or a no. If a caller can't hold, either quickly answer the person's question or take the caller's number and promise to call back as soon as possible—and be sure you do. How many times have you left your number with someone who either never returned the call or got back to you hours later? That's a great way to create a dissatisfied customer. Finally, when you put someone on hold, check back with the person as quickly and as often as possible. Apologize for the delay, give the person a status update, and always offer to call back if that's a more convenient option.

Pickup

Enterprise built its reputation on picking up customers and bringing them to their rentals. It's actually an innovation that happened by accident. As Enterprise began to create partnerships with body shops in the 1970s, it printed up business cards with a map to the nearest office. Problem was, body shop customers couldn't get to the office because they had no car. Frustrated shop managers began calling and asking if someone at

Enterprise could pick these customers up. One particularly entrepreneurial branch manager agreed to do so, even though it wasn't official corporate protocol. But what the company quickly realized was that offering this personalized shuttle service had two big advantages. It allowed the company to stagger customer arrival times at the branches, since the pickups had to be scheduled in advance. It was also a perfect way to build rapport and demonstrate service above and beyond what customers could get anywhere else, even before the rental transaction commenced.

When Enterprise Rent-A-Car employees pick up a customer, they generally do so in a four-door vehicle, to make it easy for people to get in and out. They try to arrive on time, since there's nothing worse than forcing a frustrated customer to wait around. This is a customer's first in-person impression of the company, so it's a critical moment of truth. Employees use the five-to-ten-minute ride to the branch as a way to build long-term rapport. Most of the time customers aren't in a good mood at the start of the rental. Often they've been in an accident or their car is in for a repair, and no one likes to be without their own vehicle. Enterprise employees take the time to calm customers down, let them know they are in good hands with the repair shop, and maybe even discuss what their insurance covers toward rental costs. Employees picking up someone on vacation might even point out interesting restaurants and places of interest for the customer to visit during the trip.

Branch Arrival

Depending on the location, once a customer gets to a branch, he or she may be handed off to another employee to complete the rental transaction. The new employee greets the customer with a handshake and smile, introduces himself or herself, uses the customer's name, and carefully explains all aspects of the rental process. The goal is to make the customer feel valued, welcome, and affirmed in the decision to rent from Enterprise.

Keep in mind that many Enterprise offices aren't very fancy. They are often in small, tight spaces, inside car dealerships or in nondescript strip malls. This is by design, since they are located in convenient areas where customers need them most. But it's crucial for the branch to be clean, well maintained, and easy to navigate, since first impressions are essential.

Customers size up your business within seconds. If you don't immediately win them over, you probably never will. Hotels figured this out years ago and continually train staff to wow guests within the all-important first fifteen minutes of their stay. At some hotels, if you check in and mention it's your anniversary or some other event, the front desk clerk might offer to upgrade you or even send up a goodie after you arrive in your room. DoubleTree Hotels has offered guests warm chocolate chip cookies upon check-in for twenty-five years. To create an added element of surprise, it recently retrained its staff to hand out the cookie as soon as guests arrive at the counter—before they even check in—creating a more immediate welcoming experience.

Airlines realize that starting off in a positive way at the airport will make the rest of your journey smoother, too. That's one reason they have invested so much money in building and upgrading airport lounges, to provide relaxing retreats for their most valuable customers, complete with comfortable seats, power outlets, snacks, drinks, and other amenities. The hope is that if the pre-boarding portion of your journey is enjoyable, you'll be in a better mood—and stay in that frame of mind—for the entire flight.

Winning over customers right away has gained an increased sense of importance with the rise of social media. If the experience starts off badly, you might find negative comments being posted within a matter of seconds, since people feel empowered to vent their anger in cyberspace these days. The good news is that customers are just as likely to share their delight, which is the kind of feedback you should always strive to get.

Rental Contract

Completing the rental contract can be a tricky balancing act. Employees have to gather certain facts and explain various options and procedures while remaining friendly and empathetic. Effective managers know that the key is to be courteous, say "please" and "thank you," ask only for necessary information, make regular eye contact, and avoid coming across as though they are conducting an interrogation. Among the most delicate parts of the transaction is when an employee brings up the topic of collision damage waiver coverage. This can be tricky because some customers feel adequately covered already by their own auto insurance or credit card, even though these policies often don't cover all costs. If a customer turns down Enterprise's collision damage waiver coverage, the employee has to let the renter know about the potential consequences, but must do so in a way that doesn't make the customer angry. This is where style and tone can be very important. One response might be, "In that case, keep in mind that if you get into an accident we'll have to immediately report it to your insurance carrier, and we'll charge your credit card for any deductible right away." That's perfectly factual, but it risks making the customer tense. A better approach might be to say something like this: "I certainly understand that you already feel covered, and that's fine. I would just encourage you to make sure your other policies fully protect you from all charges in the event you have an accident, because customers are sometimes surprised that they don't have full coverage. The great thing about our plan is if anything at all happens to the car, you're completely off the hook. You just drop off the vehicle and go. And we don't even report the incident to your insurance company." Again, it's basically delivering the exact same information, but the second approach is more friendly, empathetic, and convincing.

"The worst thing in the world is for a customer to have a crash and then come back and find out they're going to have to pay for all the damage," Hibbard says. "Part of what we're trying to do is train people to explain the benefits of the products we offer, and then respect the customer's decision. But we know from experience that if they do buy the collision damage waiver, they're going to be much happier in the unlikely event that something does happen. After all, people are driving very expensive vehicles, and even seemingly small repairs can be costly."

To the Car

At Alamo and National, customers generally get to pick out their own vehicles. By contrast, when someone rents from Enterprise, employees usually walk customers to the lot and may present a few options, depending on how many cars are available. They will then go around the car with the customer, checking the vehicle condition and noting any preexisting damage. They'll also offer to help demonstrate some of the vehicle's features, explain how to return it, and provide their business card so the customer can call with any questions during the rental period.

Incidentally, what a customer does with your business card after you hand it over says a lot about what they think about you and your service. If they put it in their wallet, it generally means you've made a good impression and they are likely to come back. If they stuff it in with some papers or, worse, throw it away while walking out the door, that's not a very good sign.

Callbacks

For customers renting a vehicle because their car is in the shop for some kind of repair, Enterprise Rent-A-Car employees keep on top of the progress of the repair and provide regular status updates to both insurance companies and the customer. These are referred to as "callbacks." This is another opportunity to create a favorable impression for the company, showing you've gone above and beyond the call of duty to keep the customer updated on the situation with his or her vehicle. Just as with any other telephone call, it's crucial to speak with a smile, confirm that customers are satisfied with their rental vehicle, and once again say thanks for their business.

Return of Vehicle

When returning a car, customers should get the same kind of treatment and enthusiasm they experienced when they originally picked it up. This means acknowledging them, shaking their hand, and explaining the return process. To close the transaction, employees go out to the car with the customer (or for Alamo and National there is often someone waiting to check the vehicle in), walk around to ensure there's no damage, and help them look inside for items that may have been left behind. Of course, it's also important to ask those three critical questions before the customer leaves: "How was our service? What could we have done to make your experience better? And if something was wrong, what can we do to make it up to you?"

Invitation to Return

After taking note of any feedback, it's time to drive or shuttle the customer back to the shop or airport, depending on the situation. This is a chance to once again develop a relationship and thank the customer for his or her business. Before the final drop-off, employees reinforce the benefits of doing business with the company and invite the customer to return again. It's also a chance to cross-sell other parts of the organization. For example, those who rent from Enterprise at a neighborhood location may not even know the company also offers airport rentals through all three brands, or that Enterprise also sells cars, should they be in the market for a new vehicle.

While this Cycle of Service is unique to Enterprise, given the business it is in, this general concept can serve as a model for your own organization. Think through the various moments of truth your customers experience and plot them on the graph on the next page. Then figure out how you can create similar interactions with your own customers through each of these moments, leading to the ultimate goal of having a completely satisfied and loyal lifetime customer.

YOUR COMPANY'S UNIQUE CYCLE OF SERVICE

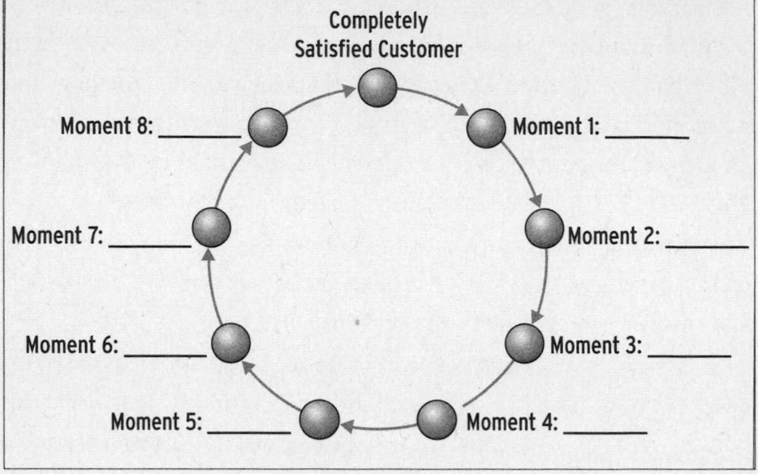

MAKE IT A GREAT DAY

Enterprise's customer service training programs for all three brands center on teaching every employee—from airport shuttle drivers to exit booth agents—how to make it a great day for each customer in a way that is appropriate given each company's brand promise. In this section, we'll let you in on these techniques.

For the most part, Alamo and National customers are either on vacation or traveling for business. Depending on the location, the first in-person interaction a customer usually has is either at a rental counter or on an airport shuttle bus. The company trains agents and drivers to immediately start sizing up customers by looking at their faces and reading their body language. Do they seem to be on vacation? Are they relaxed and happy or feeling harried? You can learn a lot simply from a person's appearance. Someone dressed in a suit with a small carry-on is very likely in town for a short business trip. A family with loads of luggage is probably arriving for a leisurely vacation. If customers have a smile on their face, they are probably happy and in a good mood. If not, chances are they had a bad experience with their flight or have experienced some other glitch along the way.

To begin delivering a great customer experience, bus drivers smile and greet customers as they board the shuttle. They assist customers with their luggage and ask whether they have rented from the company before. If not, they explain the process and answer any questions. They also offer updates on the weather, provide directions, and suggest potential points of interest. For customers on vacation, drivers ask about their plans and perhaps offer some tips for making the experience even more enjoyable based on their personal knowledge of the area.

Upon arriving at the lot, customers are welcomed by a greeter who assists with luggage, explains the process of getting a car, asks whether customers need any directions, tells them how to get out of the lot, and thanks them for renting with the company. Their final contact is with an exit booth agent, who verifies the paperwork and checks out the vehicle. This last interaction is vitally important, since it's the last impression people have about the company before they ultimately return the car. Booth agents are taught to greet customers with a smile, offer to provide directions, be speedy and efficient, and answer any questions about the return process.

Again, all of this stuff is pretty simple and seems like common sense. The big problem is that most companies fail to deliver on these basic niceties. It really does come down to things such as showing an interest in your customers, putting yourself in their shoes, anticipating their needs, making them feel special, being proactive with information, and communicating clearly. You also earn customers' loyalty when you help to eliminate any roadblocks that might cause frustration in their life. There's little Alamo, Enterprise, or National employees can do to help prevent the hiccups of air travel, from crowded planes to delayed flights and lost luggage. But they can certainly show empathy to customers who have had to deal with these issues. More important, they can help to prevent some of the frustrations that are in their control, from keeping wait times to a minimum to making sure the shuttle bus arrives at the lot in a timely manner.

CREATE A CUSTOMER-CENTRIC CULTURE

For any of this to work, you have to first know what the customer expects, and then build a commitment around exceeding these expectations that starts at the top. "It must be a message of priority directly from the CEO, and everyone has to live and breathe it daily," Gass insists. "You also need to be willing to train your entire team on how to deliver an excellent customer experience, and constantly reinforce it."

Many companies claiming to deliver great service don't really live it. It's not ingrained in their culture. "I'm convinced that a lot of companies figure that if their customer service is at least on par with everyone else, that's good enough," offers Enterprise president and chief operating officer Pam Nicholson. "We disagree. We want to go above and beyond, in order to really distinguish ourselves. And every decision we make about operating this company begins and ends with how it impacts the customer experience."

PROVIDE THE APPROPRIATE LEVEL OF TOUCH

We often hear companies talk about offering "high-touch" service. But what does this mean? Most people assume it refers to having close, personalized human interactions. However, that's not always the case. Sometimes high-touch means hands off. As you'll learn in the next chapter, Enterprise Holdings has successfully employed technology across its various brands to deliver an outstanding experience while severely limiting the amount of contact some customers have with company employees.

The trick is to understand what your customers are after. This was a bit of a learning process for Enterprise after it bought Alamo and National. The Enterprise Rent-A-Car model was built on traditional definitions of high-touch service that almost always involve human interaction through the entire Cycle of

Service. But Enterprise found that National customers were actually turned off by all that hand-holding. Most National customers are business travelers who rent cars on a frequent basis and are always in a hurry. They want to step off the plane, hop in the shuttle bus, ride to the lot, get in a car, and be on their way, making only minimal contact with employees in the process.

"We generally thought of good customer service as one where you were hugging your customers," Hibbard admits. "But we found out that if you hug a National customer, you are doing exactly the opposite of what they want or expect. Their attitude is essentially, 'Give me a car and then get out of the way.' " The same thing is essentially true of Alamo customers, though they sometimes need more personal guidance because they don't rent as often. Nevertheless, Alamo and National renters generally aren't looking for a lot of personal interaction. They want to leverage technology and get through the process quickly. "We learned pretty fast that hugging a customer doesn't always result in great customer satisfaction," Hibbard adds. "It really comes down to aligning your service with the specific expectations and aspirations of the people you serve."

DON'T ENGAGE IN GOUGING

Every business should work to enhance profitability as much as possible, just not to the detriment of the customer experience. One way to really upset customers is by overcharging them, or offering less for the money than a reasonable person would expect.

When renting a car, among the biggest customer frustrations is having to pay a premium price for fuel when returning a vehicle that has less than a full tank of gas (or whatever level it was originally delivered in). Enterprise made a commitment several years ago not to charge more than a 50 percent premium beyond the cost of gas at nearby stations in order to help defray the cost of fuel storage and related services. The maximum markup is capped at $2 per gallon. This same policy applies for Alamo and National. By contrast, many competitors have traditionally charged a premium of up to 200 percent.

The company has also been aggressive about trying to get municipalities around the country to stop imposing taxes on rental car customers to pay for various local projects. "There are some cities where taxes and fees charged by every agency from the airport to the tourism commission can hike up the cost of the rental by 40 percent or more each day," observes Lee Kaplan, Enterprise's chief administrative officer. "What we'd really like to see is a prohibition of adding excise taxes to rentals when the taxes have no direct impact on the customer. A lot of times you're paying a tax to fund a stadium that you will never even use, which doesn't seem right to us."

This principle carries through to Enterprise's car sales division. The company sells vehicles at lots around the country for a fixed price that's quite often below the average retail market price consumers might be able to find on the Internet. They've had the same one-price system in place for more than five decades. This creates a much different experience from what customers are used to. They usually expect to be greeted on the lot by a pushy salesperson who wants to haggle over price. Enterprise won't budge, even by a penny. "Jack always said, 'I don't want to fight with my customers over price,'" Andy Taylor says. The company also offers a seven-day no-questions-asked money-back guarantee and throws in a twelve-month, twelve-thousand-mile drive train warranty to give the buyer an added degree of confidence. As a result, Enterprise's car sales division has the highest ESQi score in the entire company. "I suspect that's the result of the buying experience we provide," says vice chairman Don Ross. "Our close ratio is not as high as the typical car sales operation, probably because we're not being cutthroat like some of the competition. But it goes back to what Jack taught us when we started with car sales in the 1960s. He said, 'What's important to me is when somebody comes in to talk with us, even if they don't buy a car, I want them to leave the office saying they just dealt with a really nice guy.' He treated everyone like an old friend and contended that even if the person didn't buy this time, they'd feel good about how the experience went and come back again. And they'd tell their friends, too. That's exactly how it has worked out. Once people buy a car, they return when they're ready for the next one because we've earned their loyalty."

BE WHERE CUSTOMERS NEED YOU MOST

A massive series of snowstorms in early 2010 brought much of the East Coast to a standstill. The weather was so bad, people referred to it as "Snowmageddon," as nearly three feet of snow blasted the Washington, D.C., area, shutting down the federal government for several days. Enterprise has 175 branches in and around the District of Columbia and had teams plowing snow around the clock to get cars out and make room for people to return their vehicles. At Dulles International Airport, a team of six to eight service agents worked to dig out each car by hand. It took about two hours just to clear a row of seventeen vehicles.

Beyond the work at the branches, customers on the East Coast had a hard time returning their cars. Enterprise employees had to make house calls to help shovel some of them out of the snow. At the same time, branches stayed open late to assist those who had weather-related accidents in their own vehicles and were now in need of replacement vehicles. "We helped a lot of walk-up customers from competitors that either had closed or didn't have the right kind of car available during that period," Hibbard notes.

There's no better way to earn unbending loyalty from your customers than to be there during the toughest times when they need you most. Enterprise often earns considerable goodwill by responding to disasters. Company employees worked around the clock to make cars available to stranded travelers in the days following 9/11. When any kind of natural disaster strikes, they have a fleet of Mobile Emergency Response Vehicles—or MERVs—which are essentially branches on wheels. One of the best examples of this was when Hurricane Ike barreled through

Galveston, Texas, in 2008. The Enterprise Rent-A-Car branch in town was severely damaged. Employees had to clear a forty-foot fishing pier away from the front lot and clean up about a foot of sand all around the building.

Instead of waiting to get the branch repaired, they dispatched a MERV, which was flooded with customers as soon as the thirty-two-foot bus arrived. The team at the branch faced a lot of challenges. The MERV was staffed with only three people and had no phone service for a full month. They finally got a cell phone, though it was capable of handling only one call at a time. The branch had a basic shop vacuum but no car wash or water. When a car broke down, it was impossible to fix, because every repair shop in the area was closed. And space was limited, with a lawn chair under a pop-up tent serving as the waiting area.

The local branch manager was concerned that this lack of frills would negatively impact ESQi scores. Instead, scores during that period actually rose to well above the company average. The lesson was that customers didn't care much about what kind of car they got. They just wanted reliable transportation. The attitude of the Enterprise employees was what really mattered. "We spent a lot of time just talking to our customers about what they were going through," the branch manager at the time explained. "We learned that if you simply explain things to people and make sure they understand, it goes a long way. I never had one complaint. These people had faced so many challenges, and we did everything we could to make sure that renting a car wasn't one of them."

MAKE THINGS EASY

As cash-strapped local and state governments continue to look for new ways to generate revenue, they are increasingly setting up toll roads. This can be a headache for visitors driving rental cars, since they often aren't prepared to pay these tolls and don't have loose change lying around. Worse yet, a number of tollbooths are attendant-free, so if you don't have the precise amount available, you either wind up paying too much or are subject to huge fines for passing through without paying.

To ease this frustration, Enterprise started a TollPass program. For a small fee, customers get a small device that automatically adds the cost of the toll onto their rental car bill each time they pass through. Enterprise doesn't mark up the price of these tolls and the only extra charge is a daily device fee of $2, with a maximum of $6 per rental. "We heard from customers that they wanted an easy-to-understand, efficient way to manage these tolls at a reasonable price," Hibbard says. "Our customers no longer feel forced to drive through the tollbooths without paying just because they either don't have cash on hand or didn't see anyone at the toll plaza who would take it."

SHOW EMPATHY TOWARD CUSTOMERS AS WELL

Just as it's important to lead your employees with empathy, you should also listen to your customers and their problems and respond accordingly. Showing concern can go a long way toward putting an unhappy customer into a completely different frame of mind, while creating a lasting bond. That's particularly true with Enterprise Rent-A-Car customers, since many come to the company out of a frustrating experience, especially at home-city locations.

Empathy can take many forms. For example, it's not uncommon for people to leave their wallets or other valuable items behind in rental cars. Each time a frantic customer calls Enterprise hoping to retrieve a lost item, the most crucial person in the recovery effort is the one who takes the call. These employees are taught to listen first and then express their deep concern while providing assurances that they will do whatever they can to find the missing item. They then spring into action and begin taking the necessary steps to find the misplaced goods. Sometimes it's easy and the item is already sitting at the front desk. But other times it takes a bit of detective work to trace.

Needless to say, some of the biggest smiles come from

customers who are reunited with important items that they feared might be lost for good.

DEAL FAIRLY AND HONESTLY WITH CONFLICTS

It's inevitable that you'll occasionally run into situations where pleasing an angry customer will be a real challenge. For Enterprise, this is often the case when a customer declines collision damage waiver coverage and returns a vehicle with some kind of damage. In many cases, customers deny they were responsible, or even claim the damage was already there when they checked the car out, even though it wasn't noted on any paperwork. That's when a combination of empathy, salesmanship, psychology, and negotiation all start to kick in.

"Let's say someone comes in with a missing bumper that obviously is the result of some kind of accident," Stubblefield offers. "The first thing I'd do is ask the customer if they knew what happened. If they said no, I'd offer to go check the paperwork, to see if we had any record of damage to the bumper from before. Assuming we didn't, I'd go back to the customer and say, 'I can't seem to find any record of the damage. Do you know if the bumper was on the car when you left the lot? Or did you notice it was missing?' If they respond that they did notice it was missing, I'd ask why they didn't report it. If you keep asking enough questions and the customer is at fault, they will usually admit to the problem. That's when you start to figure out how to reach an amicable resolution."

Often the damage isn't quite this extreme. Perhaps a door gets dinged, or a window comes back with a chip. In a lot of cases, the customer may truly have no idea how the damage occurred. But when you rent a car, it's your responsibility to fix the damage even if someone else causes it. In resolving such disputes, it's always best to do so in person or over the phone, not through written communications. "It's very easy to get nasty and angry when you're using email," Ross observes. "In most cases you can resolve these things just by having a reasonable discussion in person or by phone. I often used a technique that Jack Taylor taught me forty years ago. If you were to come in with a damaged car and we couldn't immediately agree on a resolution, I'd say, 'Mr. Kazanjian, what do you want? What's fair to you?' Nine out of ten times, the customer would offer up something that was pretty reasonable. If so, I'd respond, 'Okay, we can do that.' But if they suggested something that was totally out there, that we obviously couldn't accept, I'd respond, 'Oh, come on. You don't really think *that's* fair now, do you?' In most cases, they'll realize what they threw out there was unreasonable and then offer something that makes a lot more sense."

HIRE CUSTOMER-FRIENDLY EMPLOYEES

In order for your customers to have an excellent experience with your company, you've got to have employees capable of delivering top-notch service. You certainly can—and should—train them to do all of the things we've talked about in this chapter, but the process truly starts before that worker ever gets hired.

"It's something many of our groups look for in the interview process," notes Marie Artim, Enterprise's vice president of talent acquisition. "The interviews use behavioral-based interview techniques to measure each candidate's competency in this area. They really dig into what they've done in the past, and ask them to provide examples of how they have gone above and beyond. They also ask them to describe how they've dealt with difficult customers before."

We described this process in depth in Chapter 4. Here's one simple behavioral question that can help you better understand a candidate's customer service skills and experience: "Tell me about a time when you've had to deal with a difficult customer." The response should include a lot of specificity about the actions taken to achieve a positive end result. Many candidates start talking about a difficult customer, but the story ends without any kind of resolution. In such cases, it tells you the person probably didn't take the initiative to fix the situation.

Another good question is, "Give me an example of some things you've done in the past to go above and beyond when taking care of a customer." Again, specifics are key. During the interview process, you want to probe each response further. If someone says, "I had a customer who was angry with the service we provided, so I helped to turn the person around and calm them down," a logical follow-up would be, "How exactly did you do that?" Digging deeper, you might ask, "What led you to do things that way? Was there anyone else involved? Tell me more about the customer's reaction."

You should also keep a close eye on a job candidate's body language. Does the person seem frustrated while telling the story, or pleased with how he or she was able to help turn a customer's bad experience around? Nothing is foolproof, but the responses to such behavioral questions can help you to separate those with a natural ability to delight customers from those who find the whole process to be an uncomfortable chore.

Not sure how important hiring customer-focused employees is to your business? Consider this: "In terms of customer satisfaction, we've found that only a small percentage of it has to do with the car a person gets," Darrah says. "The rest depends on the employee experience, which is why hiring the right people is so important."

Why Customers Leave

Over the years, Enterprise has learned there are six primary reasons people will stop doing business with you:

- 1 percent die
- 3 percent move away
- 5 percent develop other relationships
- 9 percent leave for competitive reasons
- 14 percent are dissatisfied with the product
- 68 percent go elsewhere because of the poor way they were treated by company employees

KEYS TO DRIVING LOYALTY BY DELIVERING DAZZLING SERVICE

1. Ask customers how they feel about you through regular surveys.
2. Conduct surveys in person or by phone, keep the number of questions to a minimum, offer a satisfaction scale of no more than 1 to 5, and conclude with an opportunity to provide open-ended feedback.
3. If you have more than one location, remember that the secret to building customer loyalty is consistency from one office to another.
4. Always strive for complete satisfaction, since customers who are only somewhat satisfied are far less likely to do business with you again.
5. Hold employees accountable for exceeding customer expectations by tying bonuses in with customer service scores.
6. Look up and make eye contact with customers, and use their names as much as possible to create an instant connection.
7. Realize that sometimes less can be more when delivering good service, since a high-touch approach isn't appropriate in every situation.
8. Before customers leave, be sure to ask how they liked your service, what you could have done to make the experience better, and if there was a misstep, how you can make it up to them.
9. Empower employees at all levels to make accommodations to satisfy customers without requiring additional approval, since it's essential to address any issues immediately to prevent anyone from leaving your business angry or upset.
10. Look for ways to continually enhance the customer

experience at each moment of truth in the Cycle of Service.

11. Remember that good customer service is about the simple things, such as showing an interest in your customers, anticipating their needs, making them feel special, being proactive with information, and communicating clearly.
12. If you want your team to excel at dazzling customers, you need to train them well and on a regular basis.
13. Don't gouge customers by overcharging or adding on extra fees.
14. Be where your customers need you most, especially in difficult times.
15. Show empathy with your customers, particularly when they are unhappy, in order to build a lasting bond.
16. Try to resolve any disputes in person or over the phone, not through written communications.
17. Use behavioral interviewing techniques to identify those employees best suited to deliver great service.

7 Use Technology to Delight Customers and Employees

When Craig Kennedy first heard that Enterprise was thinking about acquiring Vanguard Holdings, owner of the Alamo and National brands, he was in a state of shock. "The first thing I did was go back to my office, sit down, stare at the wall for five minutes, and say, 'I'm not sure where to start on this thing,'" Kennedy admits.

Kennedy joined Enterprise in 1989 as a programmer and analyst. He quickly worked his way up in the technology group, ultimately becoming the company's chief information officer in 2002. As head of all technology initiatives within the company, Kennedy was essential to the success of this potential acquisition, which he first heard about not long before the deal was set to close in the summer of 2007. "If there was anyone we needed key-man insurance on at the time, it was Craig Kennedy," Enterprise CEO Andy Taylor acknowledges. In today's fast-moving world, technology is critical to making any company operate on all cylinders. It helps employees to be more productive and is increasingly used to aid in delivering an excellent customer service experience.

What initially caused Kennedy to have momentary pause wasn't the awesome responsibility ahead, or even the huge expectations that were placed on him to ensure a smooth transition.

Rather, he worried about how the acquisition might change the organization.

"We were an organic growth company. To me, it was never in the realm of possibility that we would take on an acquisition of this size," Kennedy says. But after thinking it over, Kennedy realized this could actually be an exciting opportunity for him, his team, and Enterprise. "I had watched us trying to make inroads in the airport market for a long time and being a kind of slow growth story," he adds. "This was really going to put us on the map and be a game changer." Sure, it meant moving into completely uncharted territory, but it was also an incredible challenge to show off just what technology could do to make the combined organization a huge success.

SEND PROGRAMMERS INTO THE FIELD

Enterprise has long used technology as a way to enhance efficiencies and improve overall customer service. When the company hired its first technology officer in 1973, Jack Taylor told his new hire that before he thought about writing any software programs, he first had to work in the field for nine months. Jack wanted everyone involved in technology to observe and participate in the day-to-day routine of renting cars, completing leases, and understanding the issues that employees faced. That way, coders would have a far better idea of what programs were needed, and could better build them to be more directly relevant and effective. If you didn't know what the customer experience was like when renting a car, he reasoned, how could you possibly create a program that would make the process friendlier and more efficient?

While the Enterprise technology team has grown far too large to send all new IT recruits into the field anymore, for smaller companies this same principle remains highly effective. Often computer programmers scope projects based on the technical side of what they are told a customer wants to accomplish. For instance, let's say you run a furniture store and need a program to show how much inventory of a given item is readily in stock. It's pretty easy to take a series of business requirements and build something like this. But think about how much more effective the ultimate solution would be if you first sent the programmer out to work in the field for a few days. Just knowing whether something was available might not be good enough for customers. If an item was in inventory, how much would it cost to deliver? Are there any other complementary pieces that go with it? What other details could you provide about the item, including where it came from, what materials were used to make it, and so forth? And if it's not in stock, when will the next shipment arrive? Is anything similar available for immediate delivery? By understanding all of the questions a customer might have, beyond just whether something is in stock or not, the person designing the inventory program can create a tool that is much more valuable than what you first envisioned.

Although they no longer are required to spend time out on the front lines, programmers at Enterprise remain close to their customers. The company divides the fourteen hundred members of its IT staff into application teams organized by business area. For example, there are teams devoted to serving the needs of rental, national reservations, fleet services, airport operations, and so forth. Programmers on each team work directly with liaisons from the various departments to get a deeper knowledge of the operations they support and what the specific business requirements are. This lets IT workers become subject matter experts on a particular business area and makes sure they have a clear understanding of the needs of employees, customers, and the business. It also gives the business unit liaisons a better understanding of what the IT department can do for them and fosters a stronger working relationship on all sides.

Enterprise feels it's crucial for IT professionals to work hand in hand with those closest to the business to better enable optimal solutions.

"It's very easy for companies to allow their technology people to work in a vacuum," Andy Taylor observes. "When that happens, they wind up solving technology problems instead of business problems. At the same time, nontechnical businesspeople may not understand what technology can and cannot do. That's why the two sides must work together and have a common purpose and understanding. They need to know their real reason for being is to serve the customer with technology. The goal for great technology is to enable our team members to better serve our customers."

"Never forget who your customers are," advises vice chairman Don Ross. "Some IT people feel the customer is the department head they report to, or even the business liaison they work with. The person at corporate *isn't* your most important customer. For us, the real customer is the person at the counter trying to rent a car, and the Enterprise employee helping in that process."

THINK BEYOND THE BASICS

As is the case in many businesses, Enterprise's initial foray into technology was more inwardly focused, looking at how it could automate routine functions such as accounting, payroll, and tracking inventories. Part of this had to do with the limitations of early computer systems, which were more like glorified calculators given their small memories and not-so-powerful processors. As time went on, the company realized it needed technology to help streamline various aspects of the overall operation.

Take the rental transaction itself. For years this was a purely manual process. Tickets were written by hand, cars were tracked on a chalkboard, and customer information was jotted down on plain index cards. When Enterprise first thought about automating this process, it seemed like an overwhelmingly complex endeavor. However, as the number of transactions began to rise, executives realized something had to be done, and not only to dig everyone out from under a huge pile of paperwork.

"Employees would write contracts on clipboards, not looking at customers as they gathered various bits of information,"

Andy Taylor recalls. "They made very little eye contact, which was not acceptable." So in the mid-1980s, the company decided to devote whatever resources were necessary to build systems that not only improved internal processes but also strengthened customer interactions.

The result was a system known as ECARS, an acronym for Enterprise Computer Assisted Rental System. The first version was rolled out in just a few locations to test how well it worked. It initially was used to simply open and close rental tickets. After seeing how well it worked, ECARS was introduced across the whole organization, with all of the branches connected to a database at corporate headquarters, first by telephone, then by satellite, and now through more advanced T1 lines.

As the functionality of ECARS increased, it began to integrate an early form of email that allowed employees to easily send electronic messages to one another through the system. While this sounds like common sense today, some Enterprise executives initially resisted the enhancement. They thought it was far better for employees to talk with each other directly, by phone or in person. But it quickly became apparent that this same interaction and relationship building could still take place in digital form.

"The messaging system gave all employees a chance to instantly talk to their colleagues around the world and share best practices for customer service, long before anyone even heard of email," Andy Taylor observes. "We could also send out announcements and distribute important information. As frontline employees came up with ideas for enhancing the program, they could send these suggestions directly to the ECARS programmers electronically."

The initial incarnation of ECARS was in full deployment by 1989 and has continually evolved. The system was eventually used to store customer preferences, handle complicated billing, and show which branches had specific car types. But in the early 1990s, the company made an interesting realization. It discovered that those workers most adept at inputting data into ECARS wound up getting the biggest promotions, even though all of that typing didn't necessarily improve the customer experience. In other words, it became apparent that ECARS was designed more as a customer *transaction* system, as opposed to a customer *relationship* program.

"This wasn't how it was supposed to work," Andy Taylor admits. "It turned out that people who put a lot of data into the system weren't doing a very good job of taking care of our customers."

That led to the development of ECARS 2.0, which is still in use today. Among other things, this reservation system was designed to be more intuitive, with navigation tabs that required less typing and made it easy for employees to move through the reservation process in an order of their choice based on what was most relevant to the customer. The older version had mandatory screens that prevented employees from going from one topic to another without completing all of the required information in each section.

The messaging system built into ECARS became the foundation for Enterprise's next big technological advancement, known as ARMS, short for Automated Rental Management System. ARMS, which was issued a patent in 2007, was built to help the company's insurance and body shop partners more easily manage the rental process and other aspects of claims by electronically tracking the vehicle repair process. When a policyholder gets into an accident and files a claim, the insurance adjuster can log onto ARMS and create a reservation with Enterprise that is electronically submitted to the appropriate Enterprise branch office, based on the customer's phone number or zip code, eliminating the need for any phone calls. Once the reservation is received by Enterprise, an employee contacts the customer directly to set up the details and then ARMS monitors the whole repair process online. This allows Enterprise to keep customers apprised of how their repairs are coming along and helps adjusters to gauge what is happening each step of the way. In many cases, by keeping track of the progress, ARMS allows insurance companies to reduce rental durations, therefore lowering costs and putting customers back into their own vehicles faster.

MAKE IT DECISIONS BASED ON BENEFITS

As with all technology initiatives at Enterprise, the decision to build ARMS at an initial cost of $40 million was based foremost on whether it was the right thing to do for customers and the company's business partners. "We believe that technology for its own sake is irrelevant," insists Andy Taylor. "It's only relevant if it is solving a business problem or customer service issue. It is about empowering our employees to serve our customers. And when it comes to deciding whether to go forward with an initiative, if it's something that we are convinced will lead to taking better care of our customers, it moves to the top of our priority list, usually regardless of cost."

The technology wish list in most organizations is much larger than the resources available to complete the tasks. Enterprise handles this by putting each project request through a filter that gets scored and then prioritized by a small group consisting of the same executives who set the company's overall business direction. "Looking at ROI alone doesn't always tell the story," Kennedy observes. "Over time we've developed a scorecard that looks at every potential initiative and rates it based on six different categories."

The first is *customer experience*. To what degree will the project positively impact customer satisfaction? Second is *employee satisfaction*. Is the initiative likely to make it easier for employees to do their work, and therefore make them happier with their jobs? Third is the *impact to IT costs going forward*, followed by the *risk of not doing anything*. Finally, the company looks at potential *cost savings and revenue enhancement possibilities*, along with the *competitive advantages* that could come from going forward with the project.

Everything gets scored to produce a composite result that is compared with other projects on the drawing board. The most heavily weighted scores relate to customer experience and employee satisfaction. "The IT assessment tool embodies the company's philosophy of putting customers and employees first,"

Kennedy says. "Anything that doesn't score well in those areas sinks lower on the list." That's largely because Enterprise looks at technology as a strategic asset—something that can help to strengthen the customer relationship—and not just another cost of doing business. As a result, before even asking how much a technology project will cost to undertake, executives first want to know how it's going to help improve the lives of customers and employees.

Plus, because top business leaders are part of the technology steering committee, the priorities of IT and the organization as a whole are always in full alignment. "It used to be that technology projects were all about automating something that we were doing manually, so it was pretty straightforward," Kennedy says. "It's not so simple anymore. Now we evaluate projects based on how they will help to accomplish certain business goals. The investment in IT is probably the biggest, least understood investment most companies make. This function must operate with the highest level of trust and it needs the full support of top leadership to succeed."

PLAN INTEGRATIONS THOUGHTFULLY

As he sized up the potential acquisition of Vanguard from a technology perspective, Kennedy had a lot of research to do. Though he was certainly familiar with both Alamo and National, Kennedy knew nothing about their technology platforms. "Did they have an in-house staff or was IT outsourced?" he wondered. Prior to the Vanguard acquisition, Enterprise wrote and developed all of its technology applications in-house. The company felt this was much more efficient than hiring an outside contractor who probably didn't know the first thing about the rental car business. The company believed that internal resources should be focused on building solutions that could address the specific needs of its customers and employees based on feedback from the field. Only for more routine functions, such as accounting and basic database management, did it make more sense to outsource or buy off-the-shelf programs, given that it's tough to add much value in areas where the work performed is about the same regardless of your industry.

Kennedy jumped online and started to look up every bit of public information he could find about Vanguard's technology infrastructure. He quickly determined that the company used an outside consulting firm to manage its various technology systems. "That was almost the exact opposite approach that we took at Enterprise," Kennedy says. "But from a positive perspective, it meant we didn't have to worry about merging our in-house teams or laying people off."

Alamo and National employed a software system known as Odyssey. The platform was designed to automate the entire rental car process at the airport, from keeping track of large fleets to handling coupon codes and discount vouchers, and even monitoring how well teams did at selling vehicle upgrades and additional products such as GPS devices. Enterprise never needed a program of this nature, since managing its fleet in neighborhood locations was usually as simple as looking out the window to see how many cars were parked in the lot. At airports, however, you could have up to thirty thousand vehicles in a single location, and without technology, that kind of scale is impossible to manage effectively.

As Enterprise began to formulate an integration plan, there was much to consider. Would it keep ECARS, ARMS, and Odyssey, or would at least one of these platforms be discontinued? And what about all the technology initiatives that were already in the works before the acquisition took place? It was impossible to continue with those projects while at the same time working to bring all three companies together.

The first step in the process was to clear the decks of any plans in place prior to the acquisition. President and chief operating officer Pam Nicholson told Kennedy to start with a blank slate and figure out which path made the most sense given the enduring needs of the organization as a whole.

"Frankly, we had a bunch of strategic initiatives in place before this all happened, some of which were ready to go live," admits Mike Nolfo, Enterprise's vice president of information technology. "But they were the wrong approach given what the new company looked like. So we stopped all that work without batting an eye."

Knowing that Odyssey wouldn't cease to work after the sale closed, Kennedy realized he could just keep everything moving as it had been before until he and his team had time to figure out the best path forward. They had three immediate goals: use technology to share the fleet of vehicles across all three brands, move the operations of Alamo and National into the operating group structure that Enterprise had developed over the years, and bring the employee population for the whole company together under one common system for payroll, benefits, and time recording.

"The fleet part was a bit of a challenge because all of the Enterprise groups owned their own cars, in contrast to Alamo and National, which were centralized," Kennedy explains. "We needed to be able to move cars to where the business was. So when travel was high, you could move more vehicles to the airports, and in quieter periods you would seamlessly transition them to the home-city locations. We bridged our existing system in with Vanguard's technology to make it all work."

The team took its time to build a plan for moving forward, since IT mistakes can be very expensive. "If you mess something up, it can cause the whole company to come to a standstill," Kennedy says. "IT errors are more costly than in other parts of the business, necessitating a different commitment to quality and caution than you might otherwise have. Some companies let deadlines and pressure from corporate entities press programmers into putting things into production that aren't ready, and they often pay a price for that. I think IT needs to be the strongest voice on when something is ready to be launched. Jack Taylor used to say that IT should never be the reason a company can't grow, and we live by that philosophy today. We'd rather err on the side of overbuilding before the launch, knowing we'll grow into the technology, as opposed to being caught short instead."

Over the course of about a year it was ultimately decided that ECARS would remain the rental system for Enterprise Rent-A-Car neighborhood branches, while Odyssey would be the platform for airport operations across all three brands. ARMS, meanwhile, would work across the organization, though still largely serving Enterprise Rent-A-Car, given that brand's focus on working with insurance companies and body shops. At the same time, Enterprise moved over to a hybrid model as it relates to maintaining Odyssey, outsourcing certain aspects to the vendor that created it and keeping other parts in-house.

AUTOMATE TO ENHANCE SATISFACTION

Beyond new software systems, the Vanguard acquisition allowed Enterprise to learn valuable lessons about how to use technology in new and different ways to enhance the customer experience. Enterprise previously believed that the only way to earn loyalty was through its people, by doing all the things we talked about in the previous chapter. But Alamo and National taught the company that technology could have just as big an impact on driving customer loyalty—and in some cases could be an even more powerful way to create a legion of fans for the brand. Now technology is highly targeted to accomplishing what's appropriate for each brand's unique service model.

"At Enterprise, it's important not to do things with technology that take people out of the transaction, because that's such a core piece of who we are," Kennedy says. "But that's not true at National. When I realized this and began putting on my IT hat, it opened up my mind to a world of possibilities as it related to using automation to do things we probably never would have said yes to with Enterprise as a stand-alone company."

Since its founding, Enterprise has specialized in creating a great customer experience that was facilitated by contact with employees. The belief was that the more time customers spent with these customer-focused workers throughout the whole Cycle of Service, the more satisfied those customers would be.

For Enterprise Rent-A-Car, that's still largely true. The company tends to rent to people who only need a car on occasion. In the home-city markets, these customers are usually in a bind for one reason or another (which is why their own vehicle is unavailable), and some hand-holding and caring by a friendly Enterprise employee can go a long way toward making them happy.

"For the Enterprise brand, the philosophy is that anything we can do with technology that allows the employee working with the customer to focus more on the customer and his or her needs is a good thing," Nolfo says. "We want to automate anything that's likely to divert attention away from the customer."

But that's the exact opposite of how the company thinks about technology initiatives for National and, to a large degree, Alamo. National customers are mostly business travelers who are on the road several days a month and just want to get in and out of the rental car transaction as quickly as possible. That's why the company created what it calls the Emerald Club experience. It allows members of National's frequent-renter program to simply book a car online in the midsized category or above, hop off the plane, get on the shuttle bus, choose any car on the lot, and drive off, without having to deal with a human other than the bus driver and exit booth attendant. The process is otherwise completely automated. Customers even get an email that arrives about an hour before the scheduled rental, so when they turn on their mobile phones after landing at the airport, there's a message in their inbox confirming that National is ready for them to pick up their car.

"We call it an arrival alert, and it essentially puts customers in control of the rental," says Rob Connors, National's brand manager. "We send a message saying that your car is waiting for you and offer advice on how to find the shuttle bus and so forth, in case it's an unfamiliar city. The message is simple, but it takes away any fear a customer might have about whether something went wrong with the reservation. There's nothing worse than heading to the exit gate only to be told that your name isn't in the system. These alerts send a reassuring message that we're expecting you."

While this makes customers happy, it also simplifies National's business model, since the company doesn't have to meticulously match specific cars to each customer's reservation, something that eats up a lot of extra time.

"The National customer doesn't want to engage with our people unless they have a problem," Nolfo insists. "They want to be able to move as swiftly through the process as possible. Automation tools that take people out of the transaction, remove friction, and create fewer touch points are what those customers value most."

Alamo also uses technology to automate a number of functions, though for a different purpose. Alamo customers are generally leisure travelers who still often check in with an agent. But some prefer a more self-service model. To address that, Alamo has automated kiosks that allow travelers to look up their reservations, enter coupon codes for extra discounts, check in, print maps, enter frequent-flyer program information, and purchase upgrades and extras. This is the same technology airlines have used for many years to allow passengers to check in for flights, select seats, check bags, and purchase upgrades electronically. Travelers who use the Alamo kiosks report that it saves them ten to twenty-five minutes, especially if there is a line to see an agent. Alamo also works with a number of outside travel industry partners, so automation is used to ensure that reservations made by these providers are entered into the system correctly, and that cars are ready when travelers arrive.

New advancements can also be deployed to enable shortcuts and conveniences using older technologies. For instance, American Airlines lets members of its frequent-flyer program sign up for its Remember Me telephone service. The Remember Me system keeps track of a customer's phone number, and when the customer calls in from that line on the day of the trip, he or she is automatically given a status update on the flight, without having to enter any information. Starwood Hotels is testing a new system that enables members of its Starwood Preferred Guest program to get into their hotel room using the same specially programmed keycard at every location. The room number is sent to their mobile device on the day of arrival as a text message. Retail stores are increasingly adding self-checkout lanes for shoppers who either don't want to wait in line or would rather not deal with a cranky clerk. And some banks are installing self-service kiosks and video tellers to reduce wait times and handle a greater number of routine transactions using automated devices.

Enterprise uses technology behind the scenes to facilitate the customer experience in some unique ways as well. For instance, it has GPS technology built into many shuttle buses, sending real-time tracking information on where the buses are and how often they are being used. This helps to make sure customers don't have to wait a long time to be picked up and also detects when a bus needs to be taken out of the fleet for maintenance.

THINK SPEED AND FUNCTIONALITY

For all three brands, creating a robust and user-friendly online presence is essential, since the vast majority of all reservations are now made electronically. We'll talk more about the keys to building an effective website in Chapter 8, but offering new and different ways for people to use technology even for something as straightforward as a car rental transaction is becoming increasingly important. "When we look into the future, the relationship people have with technology is changing," Kennedy observes. "Just look at the whole mobile phone movement, and how quickly people have been buying tablets. All of these devices are becoming part of the everyday consumer experience. This creates an opportunity for technology to touch our customers much more directly than was possible in the past."

Every website today needs to be optimized for use with smartphones and other mobile devices, given how ubiquitous they have become. Not only are people increasingly using smartphones to access websites, they are also using them to perform an ever-expanding number of transactions.

While it might seem basic, renting a car is a deeper transaction than simply shopping for items and putting them into an online shopping cart. You have to make a lot of decisions along the way. Where do you want to pick up the car? What time? What size car do you want? Which options? Enterprise spent months creating the right workflow, and followed that with testing and customer feedback. "We have user experience specialists on staff who monitor the Web pages where customers seem to be struggling," Kennedy shares. "They determine this by seeing which pages users either are spending a lot of time on or consistently click out of due to frustration. This tells us where we need to do some work to make these pages more navigable."

Speed is another big concern for Web users. According to research conducted by Microsoft, users will visit your site less often if it is more than 250 milliseconds, or one-quarter of a second, slower than a close competitor's. While people have more patience with graphics-intensive sites than simple searches, if a video stalls while loading or pages have so much data they take what seems like ages to load, users are likely to click away, quite possibly never to return. Keep in mind that the desire for speed is only increasing. Back in 2009, Forrester Research determined that online shoppers expected pages to load in two seconds or less. Just three years earlier, that barrier was four seconds. Now even the two-second rule is being reduced to milliseconds.

SCREEN FOR MORE THAN JUST IT SMARTS

Because of the specialized needs of the Enterprise IT department, which has a budget of more than $300 million per year, most employees are hired from the outside, as opposed to rotating in from different parts of the business. Given the specific skills one must have to be a programmer, recruiters look for people with targeted degrees, areas of experience, and coding backgrounds. However, Enterprise also seeks IT candidates with a demonstrated customer service orientation, using some of the behavioral interviewing techniques we discussed earlier.

"It's really one of the tougher things we face, because there are a lot of folks in the world with great IT skills that don't have the best interpersonal skills or aren't good communicators," Kennedy admits. "They prefer to deal with machines instead of people. But we put a high emphasis in the interview on assessing communication skills and one's orientation to customer service. Granted, there are times you need those hard-core technicians that might not be as strong in those other areas, but we really want people who can communicate and represent themselves well. They need to be able to interact with others in the business at a level everyone can comprehend, and not just by using tech terminology."

While programmers receive a competitive salary, many IT managers have a compensation package that is largely contingent upon the company's bottom line, giving them an added incentive to think like entrepreneurs and create automated solutions that drive customer and employee loyalty. All programmers are allowed to work with the latest technologies and are kept up to date through regular training. Plus, just as with the rest of the company, nearly everyone in the department is promoted from within. As a result, Enterprise's IT department has been written about by numerous publications, including *CIO* magazine, and has a retention rate of nearly 90 percent. Kennedy is only the third chief information officer in the company's history, an unusual feat in a profession known for its high turnover.

BUILD SCALE THROUGH AUTOMATION

Beyond the tangible things technology can do for your company, your employees, and your customers, it can also help to achieve breadth and efficiencies that would otherwise be out of reach. "Technology gives us scale," Kennedy says. "Given how big we are and the number of transactions we conduct on a daily basis, this could never be done manually on paper. Without automation, it would be impossible for us to have grown to the size we are today."

In addition, technology can open up new markets to distribute your goods and services. "It used to be you'd have to call us directly to make a reservation for a car," Kennedy observes. "Now through the various global distribution systems, you can make reservations electronically through a variety of different websites."

The Web makes it possible for even the smallest business to have a global presence. You can set up your own website and, depending on what you offer, also sell through a variety of other channels, including eBay and Amazon.com. The Web has changed the rules for most industries, and if you aren't taking advantage of the opportunities it provides, you are likely to be left behind. Look at what happened to Borders, the once venerable bookstore chain. The company wasn't convinced that selling through the Web would take off in a major way and got blindsided by the shift to purchasing books online and in electronic formats. The result? Borders couldn't compete with Barnes and Noble or Amazon, which had a huge leg up in these areas, and was ultimately forced out of business.

There's another big advantage technology brings to Enterprise. While the company is largely decentralized—giving each operating group the freedom to make its own decisions—automation allows everyone to operate under a common set of standards. "The IT department at Enterprise is a very centralized entity that embodies those practices that we need everybody to do the same way across the organization into the systems we build," Kennedy explains. "This unlocks the ability for our group general managers to be able to work independently of each other, and decentralized from the corporate entity, but still know that they're operating within the boundaries of what we expect. If there's something we don't want them to do, the system can be built to prevent that from happening. Having a common system that everybody is on provides a nice framework for people to make decentralized decisions while knowing that what they are doing is within what is acceptable to the company."

KEYS TO DRIVING LOYALTY BY USING TECHNOLOGY TO DELIGHT CUSTOMERS AND EMPLOYEES

1. Send members of your IT team to work out in the field before they start programming, to give them a better understanding of how to create software that most effectively meets the needs of both customers and employees.
2. Base decisions about whether to green-light any new technology initiative on whether it's the right thing to do for customers, employees, and your business partners.
3. Prioritize IT projects using a scorecard based on the following categories: (1) customer experience, (2) employee satisfaction, (3) impact to IT costs going forward, (4) the risk of not doing anything, (5) the cost savings and revenue enhancement possibilities, and (6) competitive advantages.
4. Make your top business leaders part of the IT steering committee, so the priorities of the organization are always in full alignment.
5. Don't implement any new software until it is fully ready, since IT mistakes can be very expensive.
6. Use technology to deliver excellent customer service by empowering customers and automating processes that otherwise would need to be handled by your staff.
7. Create a robust and user-friendly online presence.
8. Ensure that your website is fast and optimized for use with smartphones and other mobile devices, as customers are increasingly using these to surf the Web, access information, and perform transactions.
9. Seek to hire IT candidates with a demonstrated

customer service orientation, which you can gauge by using behavioral interviewing techniques.

10. Let technology help to bring scale and efficiencies to your business, opening up more markets than would otherwise be possible.

8 Practice Full-Spectrum Marketing

Once you've built a solid infrastructure for driving loyalty among your customers and employees and created an effective brand, you need to use full-spectrum marketing to promote and enhance the message about what your company has to offer.

At one time, marketing was pretty straightforward. The person in charge of this function was generally responsible for getting the word out through what are often referred to as the "paid" channels, namely, television, print, and online advertising, along with sponsorships and corporate websites. Most companies had a separate person on the communications side who looked after "earned" efforts, such as public relations and other word-of-mouth initiatives that require little or no direct placement costs but are completely out of your control because, at least on the PR side, you can't tell a reporter what to say or write. Sometimes the marketing and communications heads would work together, particularly when it came to joining forces on "owned" channels such as the corporate website, but often these efforts were largely siloed and run by different people.

Such a strategy no longer makes sense, as the lines between marketing and communications have increasingly become blurred. Audiences are more fragmented than ever before. At the same time, the potential channels for getting your message disseminated keep multiplying by the day. That's why you need to think about the marketing role from multiple perspectives. In essence, you want a single and consistent message that is delivered through the full spectrum of options at your disposal, emphasizing those channels most uniquely suited to reaching your target audience. The more you can get customers to engage with you through different channels, the closer the connection they will have to your company, the faster your brand will grow, and the more loyalty you will engender.

TRADITIONAL MARKETING CHANNELS AT A GLANCE

TYPE	EXAMPLES	BENEFITS	DOWNSIDES
Paid	• Advertising • Sponsorships • Paid search	• Full control • Large scale • Immediate placement	• Expensive • Less credibility • Lower response rates
Owned	• Website • Blogs • Twitter	• Cost-efficient • Easy to update • Reach niche audiences	• Tough to attract audience • Lots of competition • Not as trustworthy
Earned	• Public relations • Media placements • Word of mouth/viral	• Most credible • Long shelf life • Outside endorsement	• Difficult to get • No control of message • Can be negative

TELL YOUR STORY WELL

At its most basic level, effective marketing is good storytelling. It involves using a variety of means to communicate a cohesive message about your company. Part of that message relates to the products or services you offer, but the rest has to do with the experience, or even the benefit a consumer gets from doing business with you.

Pharmaceutical companies have become huge marketers in recent years. In fact, GlaxoSmithKline is now among the top ten advertisers in the United States in terms of overall annual spending. GlaxoSmithKline's most heavily marketed products include the asthma remedy Advair, the osteoporosis pill Boniva, the prostate medication Avodart, and the antiviral drug Valtrex. Drug makers such as GlaxoSmithKline are effective users of full-spectrum marketing. They invest millions of dollars in paid TV, print, and online advertising, plus on an array of company-owned websites to effectively promote select medications. They then use various techniques to get earned stories about the benefits of the drugs placed in a variety of media outlets, from the health segment on the nightly news to articles in various medical journals. Beyond that, they equip their sales teams with materials (company-written brochures, white papers, third-party reprints, etc.) to bring into medical offices, they sponsor events designed to reinforce the benefits of their drugs, and they partake in online discussions to ultimately convince patients to ask for the medication and encourage doctors to prescribe it. Pharmaceutical companies employ full-spectrum marketing to tell a complete story about the benefits of each drug—what it does, whom it's right for, and how it will improve your life, even after considering all of the potential side effects.

Enterprise is a big believer in the notion of full-spectrum marketing and understands the importance of cohesiveness in terms of getting its message out through multiple channels. In 2009, the company brought its marketing and communications departments together under one common structure, putting the company's former head of communications in charge of the overall effort.

"In the past, communications professionals like me specialized in having a two-way dialogue with outside folks about our company," notes Patrick Farrell, Enterprise's chief marketing and communications officer. "Today so much of marketing is a two-way dialogue because of efforts in social media and channels outside of the standard media, such as network television." Farrell, who has a journalism degree, began his career as a newspaper reporter before moving into the corporate side leading the communications effort at such consumer companies as Ralston Purina and Kraft. He joined Enterprise in 1999, holding various communications roles prior to being promoted into his current position.

Enterprise's full-spectrum marketing efforts focus on finding what Farrell describes as the "magic elixir" for each of the company's brands, or the message that will resonate most effectively through the countless communication options at his disposal.

"Before, as a marketing director you developed your radio, TV, and print spots, and then repeated that same message over and over hoping it would be memorable and that the public would fondly recall some attribute about your product," he says. "Today it's far more difficult to get your message across. You also now have customers on the Internet and otherwise constantly taking you to task for something you've done wrong in a way that is visible to millions of people. Understanding how to engage in that process involves using the combination of traditional marketing techniques combined with the skills of a communications professional." When this is done effectively, you can turn someone who is unhappy for some reason into a satisfied—or even loyal—customer by engaging quickly to solve his or her problem.

Enterprise employs different marketing channels in unique ways across its various brands, based on what resonates best with its target audiences. For instance, National relies heavily on print and TV advertising, while Alamo is marketed almost exclusively online.

"Importantly, marketing is not just advertising," Farrell advises. "It's the presentation of your product or service in all of its complexity through every channel available to you. I think that's why you'll see more and more corporations combining communications and marketing, as we have, because all of these channels must work together."

In this chapter, we'll discuss some of the most commonly

used marketing channels available, look at how they are evolving, explore the pros and cons of each, and cover the various ways they can be used to help drive loyalty for your business.

PUT IT IN PRINT

Print advertising comes in many flavors and is one of the oldest forms of marketing around. Long before television and radio were created, businesses got the word out by placing ads in newspapers, magazines, and the yellow pages. In fact, at one point you couldn't operate a successful business without having a yellow pages listing. Alamo Rent A Car got its name because the company's original founders wanted it to be listed first among car rental providers in the phone book. Today, being in the yellow pages is much less relevant. Can you remember the last time you looked something up in one of these directories? As recently as 2005, it was said that nearly 97 percent of all households had at least one copy of the local yellow pages, and 77 percent used it more than once a month. Today consumers turn to the Internet 80 percent of the time when seeking a new product or service. The yellow pages is a far more distant option.

Newspaper and magazine advertising, however, can still be highly effective, particularly when it is carefully targeted to your primary demographic. For instance, if you manage a mutual fund, placing an ad in the general section of the *New York Times* will probably do very little to increase awareness and generate additional cash flow from new shareholders. Moving that ad to the business section is a step forward and will likely lead to better results. Most effective of all would be to place your ad in the paper's special quarterly mutual fund section, where you can presume that every reader has at least some interest in fund investing. There are two caveats to consider, however. First, the number of competitors is bound to increase, since other funds will also want to advertise in this section, creating additional noise. More important, the success of any ad still comes down to the copy and design. So if you don't have a compelling message, even placing it in an ideal setting is unlikely to yield the results you seek.

While Alamo generally doesn't do much print advertising, Enterprise and National use it in very targeted ways. The two brands are often featured together in ads in industry trade publications geared to travel agents and business travel executives, with the messages focusing on the benefits and scale both companies can provide to the corporate market. "We keep the brands separate, but we market them as a joint solution," Farrell explains. "We convey the message that National is a tremendous airport provider, while Enterprise can serve your needs in the local market. The two brands complement each other, and you talk to one representative from our company to take advantage of the economies of scale of both." This has been a major benefit of the acquisition. With all three brands at its disposal, Enterprise Holdings has a bigger footprint than any other company in the car rental industry, something that is particularly attractive to corporate accounts and travel planners.

By contrast, in retail publications, the brands are always kept separate. National advertises selectively in magazines read by its target market of corporate travelers, including *Inc.*, *Fortune*, and *Golf Magazine*. These endeavors help to build brand awareness among those most likely to do business with the company, emphasizing the message that "business pros rent from National."

TARGET THROUGH TV

Advertising on television still offers the best way to reach the largest audience, but it is usually the most expensive option. Ads for the 2012 Super Bowl ran upwards of $3.5 million for a thirty-second spot. Considering that the show garnered 111 million viewers, this translated into about 3¢ for each pair of eyeballs. Trouble is, depending on what your company offers, your ad may be of very little interest to the vast majority of those viewers, making the per-person cost of your target audience significantly higher. What's more, TV advertising must be repeated over and over again. If someone happens to miss the show you advertise on, or even walks out of the room while your commercial airs, they won't hear your message. You increase your odds through repetition.

I learned this lesson years ago while working as a TV news anchor and reporter. While most people in the viewing area knew who I was, since I was on the air regularly starting at 6:00 a.m. each weekday, the average viewer missed the majority of my stories because he or she happened to not be watching at the exact moment these reports aired. My name recognition was high, because I was on TV all the time, but my specific stories weren't on the tip of every viewer's tongue because no one could possibly watch every single newscast.

As with print, TV advertising should be carefully targeted to your particular demographic. With all of the niche cable outlets today, reaching specific groups has become easier and more cost effective than ever. That's exactly how Enterprise puts its TV ad dollars to work. The company uses this precious thirty seconds of airtime to convey the experience of both customers *and* employees of the company's brands.

Years ago, Enterprise Rent-A-Car regularly ran ads on national TV, trumpeting the company's "pick you up" service. You might remember the car driving down the road wrapped up like a parcel? Today the focus of these ads has shifted.

"What became apparent to me was the thing that was missing from our commercials was what really made the Enterprise brand so special: the people who work here," Farrell says. "When you rent from us, there's a certain energy that comes through from our people. Everybody is dressed professionally, they've got a smile on their face, they're willing to do just about anything to earn your satisfaction."

This realization formed the basis of an advertising campaign that the company calls "The Enterprise Way."

"The ad series speaks to the customer first, by showing the key attributes that make us different from the competition," Farrell explains. "But it's also meant to reinforce to our own employees what we stand for. There's a big part of 'The Enterprise

Way' campaign that is designed to say to our own folks, 'This is how we do things around here.' It demonstrates the attributes of this company that need to be portrayed on a daily basis."

The ads feature Enterprise employees and emphasize that the company is family owned. They send a clear message that Enterprise Rent-A-Car employees are bright, professionally dressed, engaged, entrepreneurial, empowered, and customer-focused. "Most marketers have to come up with a story and then go back to company executives and say, 'This is what the customer wants. How can we deliver it?' " observes Jim Stoeppler, Enterprise's brand director. "We were in a position where we already provided what the customers wanted. We just had to shine a light on it."

National takes a slightly different route. The brand's primary emphasis is on earning corporate accounts. To help build its brand recognition as the premier car rental provider for business travelers, National places ads on networks most likely to be viewed by company decision makers, such as CNBC, CNN, and some of the sports channels. Each ad in the campaign features a single business traveler walking through the airport and onto the National lot with ease. A voice-over by actor Patrick Stewart points out that seasoned business pros rent from National because it is the only car rental company to "let you choose any car in the aisle and go," taking a full-sized or above vehicle yet still paying only the price for a midsized one. At the end of the ad, the traveler smiles with satisfaction and proudly says aloud something along the lines of "I deserve this" or "I can get used to this." The goal in running these ads is less about getting viewers to pick up the phone to book a car right away and more about building brand awareness so that when a National salesperson talks to a corporate account decision maker about doing business with the company, he or she will be familiar with National's brand promise and view it as the premier provider for experienced travelers.

"We are trying to convey the image of our typical customer in these ads," notes Rob Connors, who oversees branding for National Car Rental. "When you travel a lot, you're used to certain things. You get in the short security line, you stay on the executive floor at the hotel, and when you pick up your car rental you want to be the one running the show."

National's former owners spent very little on consumer media, so building brand awareness was an investment Enterprise determined was worth the cost. "The National campaign has performed very well for us," Farrell says. "It really lifted our brand reputation in a big way. We went from a place where choice was not really attributed to any one particular car rental company to where National clearly has emerged as the leader in this space."

By contrast, Alamo does almost no television advertising, other than to support a handful of corporate sponsorships. The company feels its dollars are better spent on Web advertising and other online endeavors, given that its customer base is more interested in finding the lowest possible price, which is often done by surfing online.

While television still has huge potential, companies should think long and hard before committing to any kind of TV ad campaign. It's not always the best or most cost-effective option along the marketing spectrum. If you decide to undertake a TV campaign, make certain you have an adequate budget to keep repeating the ad for a sufficient period—at least thirty days, but probably a lot longer. You also need to figure in the cost of production. Above all, ensure that you are targeting the right audience. If you want to reach young adults across America, perhaps a thirty-second spot on *American Idol* makes sense. But if you're looking for business closer to home, you can try one of the commercial broadcast channels in your local area, or perhaps a national cable network that only plays the ad in your neighborhood (you can set this up through your cable provider).

As with any endeavor of this nature, you want to test your ad to make sure it gets the appropriate response. If not, you should either tweak the message or rethink whether such marketing makes sense for your particular business. Most important, you need to craft a message that reflects the essence of what your company does and what makes it unique, while getting viewers excited about the prospect of doing business with you.

REACH CUSTOMERS THROUGH THE MAIL

Direct mail was once a very effective means of reaching a particular target market. It still can be. With all of the emails going out today, getting an interesting piece in the mail has the potential to really grab a recipient's attention. The U.S. Postal Service, struggling in the face of lower mail volumes, is working overtime to accommodate those businesses interested in using direct mail because the organization gets the vast majority of its revenue through commercial customers. The advantage of direct mail is that you can gear your list to a pinpointed demographic or reach an entire neighborhood with relative ease. Direct mail is not cheap and generally works best for higher-ticket items.

Direct mail is a numbers game. You can usually count on getting a 1 to 3 percent response rate on a well-crafted campaign, so plan your expenses accordingly to ensure that this channel makes sense.

For example, let's say you're in the business of preparing tax returns for an average of $150 each. If you mail out ten thousand professionally created pieces to your target audience, you can expect to get anywhere from one hundred to three hundred new customers as a result of this campaign. If you estimate the cost of each piece to be around 50¢, this means you can anticipate $15,000 to $45,000 in new business from the mailing. Since the up-front cost is around $5,000, that's not a bad return on investment. But let's say you instead sell frozen yogurt for an average ticket of $4. In this case you could probably get by with a simple postcard mailing for around 28¢ each. That same mailing to ten thousand would run you $2,800, though the expected revenue is much less, only $400 to $1,200. In this case, with such a low-ticket item, direct mail is a pretty poor investment.

Enterprise once did a decent amount of direct mail, offering low-cost weekend specials to customers near its home-city offices. But as online marketing became more prevalent, the company moved away from direct mail and now rarely uses it for any of its brands.

"Direct mail has a very small place in our world compared to what it used to be," Farrell says. "As with the yellow pages, we still use it, but in a much diminished way. It's a matter of understanding that the ways in which individuals receive information have shifted."

It's true that sending communications by email makes more financial sense, and frankly is the method of communication preferred by most customers these days. But direct mail may still have a place in your full-spectrum marketing arsenal. The most effective forms of direct mail fall into one of three categories: coupons, compelling letters, and what I like to call "loyalty extras."

Coupons are pretty self-explanatory. If you have a business that lends itself to offering some kind of coupon, direct mail is a good way to deliver it. However, as noted in the example above, it can be pretty expensive if you have a low-ticket item. In such cases, going with a bundled coupon approach, where you are one of many coupons in a packet, is far more cost-effective.

The second category involves sending a compelling letter about your product or service that quickly grabs the reader's attention and inspires a call to action. Some of the best material for such letters—and for the rest of your marketing efforts—can come from talking to your existing customers. Better yet, including an endorsement from a current customer in the piece can be a powerful motivator.

Freelance direct mail writer Pat Friesen often interviews customers of her clients to come up with inspiration for the letters she puts together. An interview with a customer of tour operator Maupintour led to the letter on the following page, which went out with some of the company's brochures and resulted in a much higher than normal response rate. "The letter directly introduced Maupintour, gave a sense of what a traveler could expect, and addressed the recipient's potential fear of spending thousands of dollars with an unknown company for a trip of a lifetime," Friesen explains.

Interviewing customers can provide powerful copy for all of your campaigns, not just direct mail pieces. Here are some strategies for conducting customer interviews:

1. Prepare a list of questions in advance.
2. Mention up-front how long the interview will take.
3. Listen carefully to the responses, and follow up as appropriate.
4. Tell the customer you want to hear both positive and negative comments.
5. Explain how the comments might be used, and let the

WR

Captain William H. Rush, United States Navy (Ret.)

Dear Fellow Traveler,

We just returned from our first trip with Maupintour and I'm very high on them. On a scale of 1 to 10, I'd definitely give them a 10!

Like you, my wife and I enjoy traveling. We've traveled on our own as well as been on many cruises and tours. We've seen the world!

While this was our first Maupintour vacation, I can guarantee you it won't be our last. In fact, we'd barely gotten home when my wife was asking me, "We're going to go with Maupintour again, aren't we?"

Since you're considering your first Maupintour (just as we did not too long ago), here's something you should know. I did my homework.

Because we've taken tours before that were major mistakes, this time I checked with travel offices at three Navy bases. I also talked to friends who had traveled with Maupintour. I asked my travel agent. My wife read about the company in her favorite travel magazines. Every one of these sources said basically the same thing, "Maupintour is one of the best tour groups in the world!"

And now we can confirm it from personal experience, Maupintour is THE best. The itinerary, the guides, the hotels and meals, the people on the tour ... it was a quality trip. As I told my wife, "We hit a gold mine with Maupintour."

Would I recommend them to others? I already have. Would I recommend them to you? Absolutely!

Cordially,

William H. Rush (Captain, U.S.N., Ret.)

P.S. I understand that Maupintour is very selective about their tour escorts, personally interviewing each one. You can tell the difference.

customer know he or she will have an opportunity to review anything before it goes to print.

6. Thank the customer for his or her time.
7. Follow up with a handwritten note of appreciation, to demonstrate how much you valued the customer's perspective.
8. Write up the comments you'd like to use and send them to the customer for review and approval as soon as possible after the interview.
9. If appropriate, include a release form for the customer to sign, giving you permission to use such comments as part of your full-spectrum marketing campaign.

Finally, direct mail can work well for sending loyalty extras. These are the added special touches for your best customers—and even your employees—that go out in addition to all the normal electronic communications you have with them on a regular basis.

I'm a member of numerous airline frequent-flyer programs, and all bombard my email box with messages, most of which are unwelcome since they contain little more than promotional fluff. But once a year, Southwest Airlines sends me a hard-copy birthday card in the mail. It looks pretty cheesy, but what else would you expect from Southwest Airlines? It plays along with the company's fun and friendly branding theme and is signed by executives of its Rapid Rewards program. I put the card up on my table along with the others I get from friends and family, and it reminds me of the airline every time I see it. This gets a lot more attention than an electronic card would. Likewise, how many companies send birthday cards to their employees? Probably none that you've ever worked for. But think of how powerful it would be for your employees to arrive home from work, get the mail, and find a card from you—their employer—wishing them a happy birthday, anniversary, or whatever. Loyalty extras such as these cost mere pennies but are bound to result in immeasurable goodwill. Plus there's no better time to touch customers or employees than on a special occasion, such as a birthday, since you'll be reaching them at a time when they are more likely to be in a good mood and grateful that you thought of them.

When thinking about a potential direct mail campaign, remember the Rule of 40-40-20. While not an exact science by any means, this rule states that 40 percent of direct mail success rests on having a well-targeted mailing list, another 40 percent on your offer, and the remaining 20 percent on the cleverness of the overall design and packaging.

BE VISIBLE ON THE WEB

In today's world, having a website is not an option. It's an essential component in your full-spectrum marketing arsenal and a required cost of doing business. Regardless of your industry, if you're not easy to find on the Web, you'll have a hard time keeping up with the competition. This is true both for you as an individual and for your company. Wonder whether you have enough of an online presence? Here's a simple test: go to Google and type in either your name or your company's name. If you don't get at least a full page of hits (and ideally many more) for both, there's a lot more work to be done.

Depending on your business, your website may be more informational or transactional in nature. If you offer a more personalized service, it's likely your website will serve primarily to build your credibility, engage your customers, and provide a way for people to get in contact with you. If you sell products or, as in the case of Enterprise, offer something that can be easily booked online, you'll want a site that allows customers to quickly and easily complete a transaction.

Alamo was the first car rental brand to have an Internet site. Enterprise and National both get the vast majority of all bookings through the Web as well.

"If you go back not that many years, most customers made contact with us through an 800 number. Today more people do business with us through the website than by phone," Farrell observes. "Transactions are increasingly being done using mobile devices, as well. You have to really keep up because as the world migrates to using apps, your standard website will become less relevant."

This demonstrates the importance of not only having a website but also understanding how people are accessing information about your company online, including what devices they are using. A few years back I built a new website for a company at which I was head of marketing. The site design relied heavily on Flash images to create an interactive experience. As we got ready to launch, the website development company warned me that iPhone and iPad users wouldn't be able to see any of the Flash graphics, since they weren't compatible with Apple products. The first version of the iPad had just come out, so I figured that wasn't a big deal. "This site was created for people using a desktop computer, not a mobile device," I assured the developer.

Within minutes of launching our site, two members of our sales team came barging into my office. "We can't see anything on the home page. Is something wrong with the site?" they wondered. Nothing was wrong, except they were trying to access it using their iPads, which couldn't detect the Flash images. Tablets and smartphones were clearly gaining fast, widespread adoption and we had to change our model to address this new reality. I immediately got on the phone and asked our developer to replace those Flash images right away. The old way of building sites just for people on PCs had forever lost all relevance.

There are plenty of good books on how to create an effective website, so I won't try to cover that topic in depth here. But I will offer some general guidance beyond reminding you to make sure people can access your site in many different ways.

First, when writing copy, always keep the customer in mind. This means using "you" much more frequently than "we" when talking about what you do on your site. Always think benefits over features and put yourself in the customer's shoes when preparing the content and framing the navigation. What type of information would *you* like to see about your company if you were a user on the site? What questions would you have? How would you logically categorize information and make the site easy to navigate?

Second, give customers and potential job candidates an easy way to get in touch with you. List various methods for making contact, including by phone, in person, and by email. If you invite people to submit questions or comments through your site (which you should), be sure to have someone monitoring the inbox and respond to these messages immediately. There's nothing more frustrating to a customer than submitting a comment through a website and then hearing absolutely nothing back. A customer who is angry to begin with will only get more frustrated if he or she feels you are not responding in a timely fashion—or at all.

Chobani, the Greek yogurt company I introduced you to in Chapter 1, understands this. Not long ago I opened a container of the company's yogurt during lunch, only to find some mold on top. The expiration date on the label was a good two weeks away, so I was pretty upset that I had to throw this out. I immediately went to the company's website and found a link for submitting comments. I fired off a short email about my experience, pointing out that I was a loyal customer and expressing disappointment at discovering that my recently purchased yogurt was spoiled. Within thirty minutes I had a response in my inbox from a company representative personally apologizing for what happened (not just a form response, as you get from some companies) and explaining that because the company's yogurt has no preservatives, if it ever falls below a certain temperature, mold can develop. The writer from Chobani surmised that perhaps the store I bought it from somehow didn't keep my container cold enough at some point during the process, and promised to look into the matter further (even though that would do me little good at this point). In the meantime, the email noted, I should be on the lookout in my mailbox for a token of thanks for being such a loyal customer. About a week later, I got a note of apology signed by a member of the company's customer loyalty team, plus coupons for three free yogurts of my choice. Do you think I got over my frustration with finding that mold? Absolutely. Had I not heard anything back from the company, who knows? There are plenty of other yogurt options, and I might have decided to try a different brand.

Third, include your website's URL in all of your marketing materials, using both the actual address and a QR code. QR (short for "quick response") codes are square bar-code-like symbols that act as a hyperlink when scanned by a smartphone. They automatically direct users to a particular URL. Enterprise Holdings has put QR codes inside all of its vehicles so that customers interested in getting more details about the car can simply scan the code into their smartphone. The thinking is that many people considering a certain model often rent it first to see how well they like the way the vehicle drives. By scanning the QR code, which is placed on key tags and driver's-side windows, customers can quickly access additional information about the car and even find the location of a nearby dealer.

QR codes are easy to create. Just go to Google and type in "QR code generator" for a list of free devices you can use to instantly make your own codes. All you have to do is type in the URL of the Web page you want the code to link to and the site will generate a unique QR code for you to use. Sometimes you might want to send users to your home page. Other times you'll want to direct them to more specific parts of the site. QR codes can be downloaded and integrated into all of your other marketing materials, including ads, brochures, and business cards. To see how it works, just scan the QR code below with your smartphone right now. (You'll need to download a QR code reading app first, which can be readily found for free online.)

Scan this QR code into your smartphone for instant access to the *Driving Loyalty* website.

If appropriate, you may also want to steer part of your full-spectrum marketing budget to online and paid search advertising. "We spend most of the advertising dollars for Alamo online, putting banner ads in places where we know people might be looking for a bargain car rental, such as some of the budget travel sites," Farrell shares. "We know we can do our best work for this brand by putting an offer in front of a shopper at the time they are looking for our product."

As with any other type of advertising, proper targeting and effective copy are essential ingredients to getting a good response. The Web allows you to pinpoint specific audiences better than any other channel available today.

HAVE AN INTERACTIVE ONLINE DISCUSSION

While you can completely control the content of your own website and any paid advertising messages, that's not true in the world of social media. Sites such as Facebook, Twitter, YouTube, LinkedIn, Pinterest, and even personal blogs foster two-way communications between a company and its customers. These outlets are forces you will have to reckon with whether you want to or not. Facebook has more than 845 million active users who each post an average of ninety pieces of content a month. Twitter's 600 million registered users send out tens of millions of tweets a day. YouTube has some 800 million unique monthly visitors who upload more content each month than the three major U.S. television networks combined created in the previous six decades. LinkedIn has more than 150 million members in more than two hundred countries and territories. Pinterest is the newest social media site but has been growing fast, attracting millions of members since its founding in 2009. And there are more blogs out there than you can possibly count. Anyone who can breathe can start a blog or build a page on these sites for free. My cat is even a member of both Facebook and LinkedIn!

According to Nielsen, 23 percent of all time spent on the Web today is devoted to communicating through some kind of social media. All of these sites also allow for commercial pages, meaning you can build a presence for your business as well. Again, volumes have been written on how to create effective blogs or pages on the various social media sites, so we won't cover that ground here. What we'll focus on instead is how to use social media as a way to learn more about your customers and ultimately drive their loyalty.

PRIMARY AIMS FOR HAVING A SOCIAL MEDIA PRESENCE

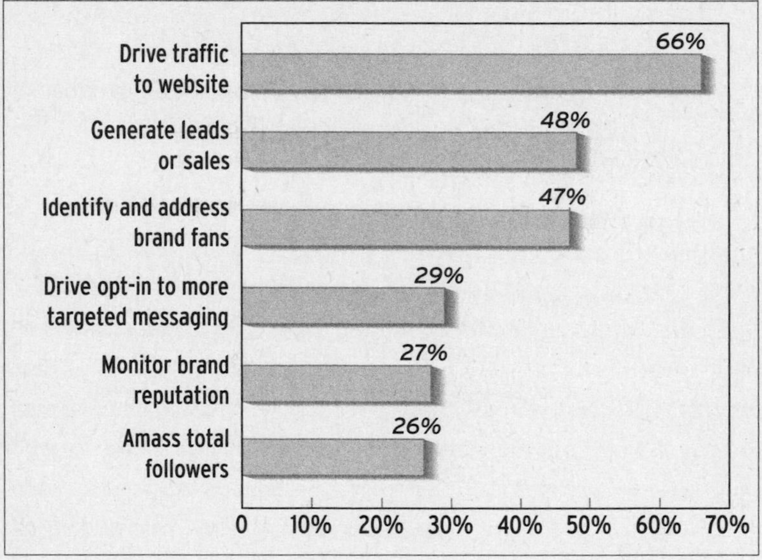

Source: Chief Marketer, www.chiefmarketer.com

The first question is whether you should have a presence on the various social media sites to begin with. The answer is probably, but it really depends on what you do. Nearly every professional could have a Facebook and LinkedIn page, but it might not be appropriate for you to post videos to YouTube or send out Twitter messages. In general, however, you should at least stake out real estate on all of these domains by reserving a name for your company. Given how many members these sites have, and the fact that it generally costs nothing to establish a presence, you have little to lose, other than the time it takes to establish and maintain these pages.

Once you take the plunge, keep in mind that the terms of engagement for social media are very different from your regular website. Social media demands back-and-forth dialogue, which means letting customers post comments—good and bad—and creating an interactive experience. If done well, these discussions can be very beneficial to the business.

"In the past, we'd have to conduct focus groups all over the place to get inside the minds of our customers," Farrell notes. "Now we have a loyal group of people from around the country who belong to the Emerald Club, for instance, and have agreed to be part of our National Facebook online community. We are able to engage them and get great insights from their feedback. In some cases we'll actually say on our page that we're thinking of doing X, Y, or Z and they'll let us know if that's something of value."

Enterprise, Alamo, and National all have a presence on the major social media sites, but the greatest emphasis to this point has been on Facebook. "Facebook is about having a spontaneous dialogue that is of value to both parties," Farrell adds. "You must be willing to have an open conversation in front of God and everybody about your product or service. If you do it well, it can drive business because people start to trust you as they see how you conduct yourself and realize you live your marketing message."

National uses its Facebook presence to converse with fellow road warriors. "We try to put some engaging content on there that a business traveler might be interested in, since that is more likely to attract a broader audience," Connors says. "For instance, we had one contest where we asked people to tell us their tales from the road and the best stories won some frequent-flyer miles. We do a lot to try to engage the audience." Rewards like this can be an effective way to encourage engagement, though what you offer must be compelling in order to get customers to take the time to participate.

Alamo's Facebook site is more lighthearted and focuses on

helping users find better values during their travels. The Enterprise Facebook page has links to some of the company's promotional material and, like the other two brands, also runs occasional contests. "Around the holidays we had a charity card on the site and gave people a chance to vote on which charities we ultimately donated money to," Stoeppler says. "We also had a thank-you contest where we asked people to tell us what kept them coming back to Enterprise. We received more than sixty-five hundred unique responses from loyal customers talking about the great service they got at our branch locations. It was more successful than we even imagined, and we more than doubled our number of fans during the promotional window."

An increasing number of corporate sites rely on fictional personalities to engage in conversations with users. For instance, Progressive Insurance has Flo, the perky salesclerk who became famous through her appearances in the company's television commercials. Flo has her own Facebook page to interact with the public. She had three and a half million fans at last count. Flo also posts comments about the company's products and discusses everything from poetry she's written to her tips for being a snazzy dresser. While Flo is a human corporate mascot, AFLAC's duck has more than 350,000 fans and manages to type out regular messages and engage in dialogues, as does the GEICO gecko, with nearly 250,000 fans.

While some companies are primarily focused just on the number of fans or likes they can gather on Facebook (or connections on LinkedIn or followers on Twitter), Stoeppler says quality is more important than quantity. "Do I want five million Facebook fans? Sure," Stoeppler admits. "Do I want five million fans but only ten thousand who care? Probably not. There's got to be a balance. Why are you a fan? Why are you following us? What do you care about? We've got to make sure we're engaging users properly. While our fan base isn't as large as some consumer companies, it is very vibrant. Our fans are tremendous advocates for the brand and those are the people we want to be connected with." Indeed, turning fans and likes into advocates who regularly interact with your brand and tell their friends about you through postings and other forms of positive feedback is how you should measure the effectiveness of your marketing efforts on Facebook and other social media sites.

WHY COMPANIES RUN SOCIAL MEDIA CAMPAIGNS

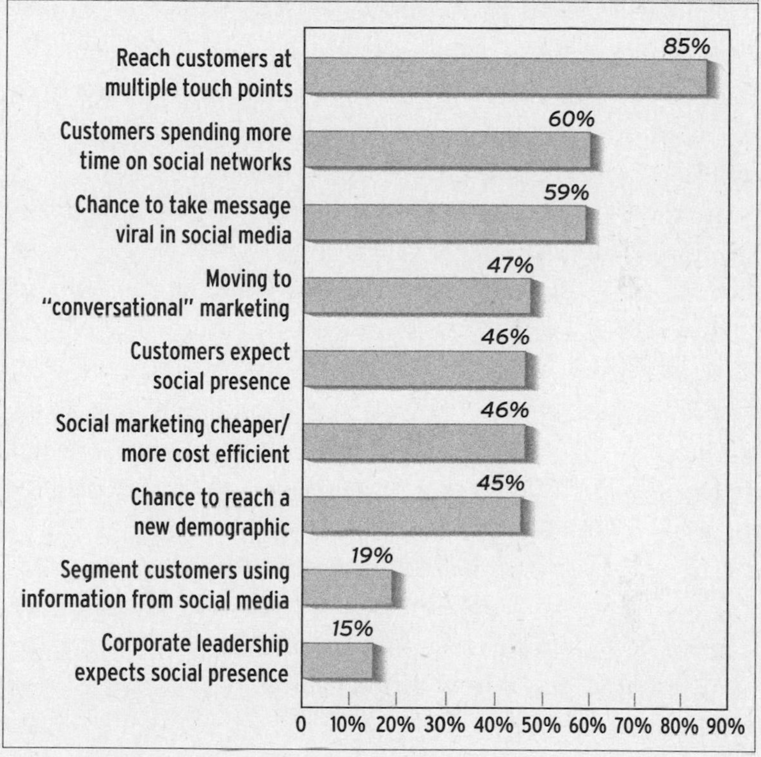

Source: Chief Marketer, www.chiefmarketer.com

When you allow users to comment on your site, remember that not every posting will be positive. "When we first launched on Facebook, most people were either looking for discounts or talking about bad service experiences," Stoeppler admits. "As we've matured in our knowledge of how to use social media and grown the fan base, the sentiment has changed and become much more positive. We still have negative comments on our pages, but we also have customer service representatives attempting to resolve those issues on the page, as well as customer brand advocates posting about positive experiences. You have to be authentic and honest on these sites or else you'll lose credibility."

The way you respond to what people are saying on social media sites plays a crucial role in determining whether you end up with loyal customers or a royal problem. Today, many customers can vent their frustrations to tens of thousands or even millions of people using Facebook, Twitter, or any of the other social media sites. They have the same potential platform on the World Wide Web that you do. Enterprise wants to know what people are saying, and if it's not positive, they will take immediate steps to resolve the issue.

"We use a service that scans the entire Web looking at what's being said about our brands in real time," Farrell shares. "If we spot a customer having a difficult experience, we can have an agent in our call center engage with them immediately. You'd be surprised how often we can quickly resolve issues and then have a once frustrated customer go back online to talk about how great we were at taking care of the situation." But in order to do so, you must be aware of what is being said about you in the social media space at all times.

Of course, you hope to delight customers consistently so that they don't resort to complaining online in the first place. But by keeping an eye out for what's being said about your company through various social media sites, you can help to protect your brand's reputation.

"We're primarily using Twitter to address customer service issues," Stoeppler says. In fact, the Twitter handles for the company's brands reflect this strategy of using the service as a way to build customer relationships: @enterprisecares, @alamocares, and @nationalcares.

Enterprise has a specialized team in St. Louis monitoring what people are saying about the brands in cyberspace. Every comment gets noticed, whether it's good or bad. The positive ones are generally forwarded to the operating group responsible for this praise. Anything vulgar gets ignored. But if someone has a legitimate issue that needs to be resolved, a member of the social media team will send a public message inviting the customer to continue the conversation offline. You never want to resolve an issue through a site discussion. "When someone is having an issue and writes about it on Twitter, we can reach out to them immediately," Stoeppler says. "We ask them to send us their contact information so we can get the issue resolved. It's what we refer to as proactive customer service."

The goal is to build a more personal relationship by phone or email. In a lot of cases, when the situation finally gets resolved in a favorable manner for both sides, your customer will post a follow-up comment praising your response.

HOW COMPANIES MEASURE SOCIAL MEDIA MARKETING SUCCESS

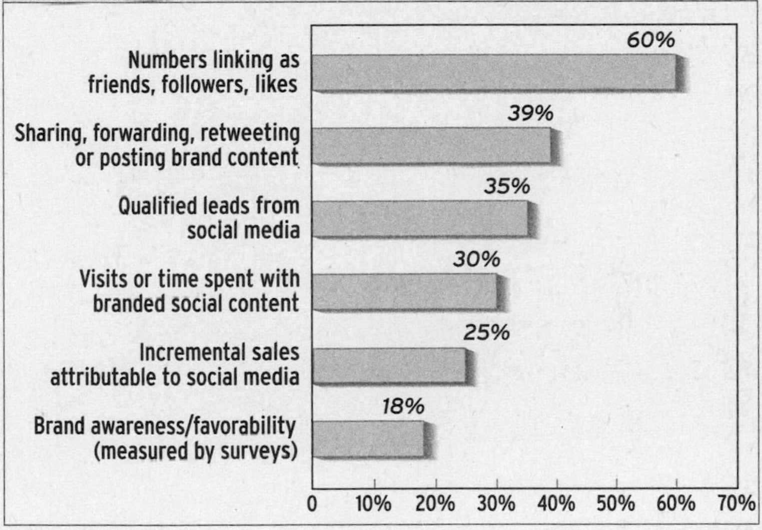

Source: Chief Marketer, www.chiefmarketer.com

If you have a visual product or service and target a female audience, Pinterest is one site you should explore. The site believes that a picture is worth a thousand words and lets users—and companies—pin up photos on what amounts to a world of online scrapbooks. Others can "follow" you, just like on Facebook and Twitter, and are able to re-pin items from your board onto theirs, thus spreading your message and images to their friends. In just a short time, Pinterest has become the third-most-popular social media networking site, ranking just behind Facebook and Twitter, with an audience that is estimated to be 85 percent women.

TOP GOALS CITED BY COMPANIES REGARDING THEIR SOCIAL MEDIA STRATEGIES

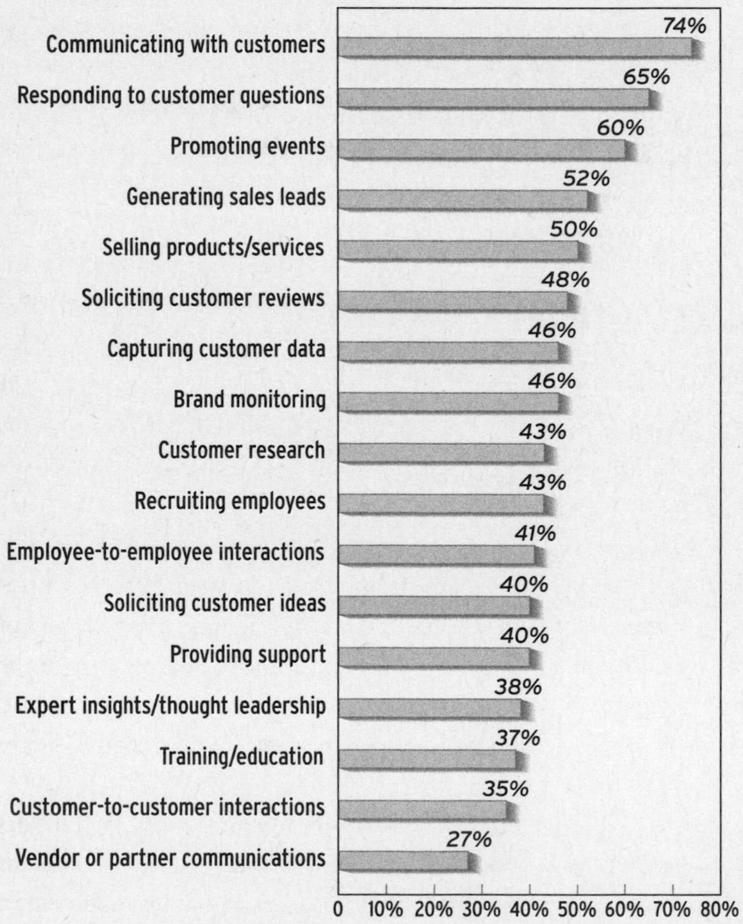

Source: IBM Institute for Business Value, "From Social Media to Social CRM: Reinventing the Customer Relationship."

INSTILL LOYALTY THROUGH MEMBER PROGRAMS

It should come as no surprise that one of the most effective ways to drive loyalty is by offering customers membership in a company loyalty program. But how many times have you signed up for a program and found that it didn't provide the kind of value you expected? The most successful loyalty programs are designed to thank frequent customers for their business, while making their experience with your company easier and more streamlined. Ideally, the program also provides rewards that are relevant, of interest to your customers, and easy to redeem. If you fail to live up to these expectations, you might wind up not driving loyalty, but rather having the opposite effect.

Today's airline loyalty programs demonstrate both sides of this equation. Ever since American Airlines introduced its AAdvantage program in 1981, nearly every carrier has given travelers a way to earn points both in the air and through spending money on affinity credit cards or even shopping with selected merchants. If you rack up enough miles, membership has special privileges beyond free flights, such as the ability to go through expedited security lines, boarding the aircraft early, getting upgraded to first class, or checking your bags for free. Trouble is, in recent years it's become harder than ever to use those frequent-flyer points you've worked so hard to build. Airlines make fewer reward seats available and upgrades of any kind nearly impossible to come by. If you're going to offer members of your loyalty program points good for goods and services, make it easy for them to redeem. Otherwise, you could instead wind up with angry and disloyal customers, as many of the airlines are starting to discover.

When run correctly, loyalty programs can have huge benefits for your business, including providing a ready-made database of prime email contacts that you can market to on a regular basis. Remember, loyalty program members are already engaged with your company at some level, or else they never would have joined the program in the first place. You can use various marketing techniques to strengthen these relationships, while generating additional business. What's more, research shows that 82 percent of affluent customers belong to loyalty programs, compared to 74 percent of the general population. So the people who will spend the most with your business are also the most likely to want to sign up.

Enterprise Holdings has loyalty programs for all three of its brands. The largest is Enterprise Plus, which was launched in 2007 and now has more than six million members. Enterprise Plus originally served as a way to automatically store information and speed frequent customers through the rental process. "When the program was initially launched, we had a lot of research that concluded Enterprise renters were different," Stoeppler says. "They didn't rent that often, since a person only gets into an accident once every seven years or so. So we didn't think it made sense to offer a frequent-renter program with rewards or other perks."

But that changed in 2011 after the company looked at a different set of statistics.

"We realized that we do have a frequent-renter population," Stoeppler shares. "It's a small percentage, but with the tremendous size of our customer base, it's still worth a great deal of annual revenue. We soon determined that offering a frequent-renter program would be meaningful to these people and help to solidify their loyalty, which is why we made the change."

In 2011, the program was enhanced to reflect its growing airport presence, while awarding points for each rental and allowing customers to earn free days and upgrades. "We found through going out and meeting with customers that offering a loyalty program and rewarding them with free days made it much more likely that they would use us for both on and off the airport," Farrell says. "When you reward customers for their loyalty, they are much less likely to do business with a competitor."

The most recent change to Enterprise Plus allows members to earn and redeem points across both the Enterprise and National brands, similar to an airline alliance.

National's Emerald Club has more than one million active

members. It allows members to earn free days or frequent-flyer points. "The program was built around the habits of frequent travelers who are used to similar programs from airlines and hotels," Connors says. The average Emerald Club member rents from National an average of five times a year, with many renting four times that amount. "These are heavy-duty users who appreciate the speed, choice, and control they get from us," Connors adds.

Alamo has a different kind of loyalty club, called Alamo Insiders. "Our members are deal hunters who get regular emails with coupons and other information showing how they can save money on their next car rental," says brand vice president John MacDonald. "They can enter their club number when booking a reservation and we'll give them our best rates available. We'll also pre-populate all of your information to save time in making the reservation."

REACH OUT THROUGH SMART EMAILS

All three programs market to members primarily through regular emails. "We let our members stay in control of the messaging they receive. We try to be on point with what they want. So, instead of just sending everyone a weekly email, we let them dictate the frequency," MacDonald observes. For instance, Emerald Club members get a monthly statement detailing recent account activity, the number of airline miles awarded, and how many free days they have earned. Alamo emails its members every Wednesday with the company's latest deals. Enterprise sends out messages only periodically, usually with some sort of special offer. In all cases, the company allows members to dictate the types of messages and frequency of these emails, from "contact me all the time" to "send me nothing at all."

"If we want to keep customers engaged and avoid any chance of them opting out, the messages really have to be on point and help them to stay in control," Connors says. "If we can't do that, we know we're going to lose you."

The company also tries to pinpoint its email messaging based on the customer's individual profile. "If you are a typical Enterprise home-city renter, we might give you an offer to rent at the airport," Stoeppler says. "If you're a corporate renter but never rented from us on the weekend to take your family on vacation, we'll send a message suggesting you try that, and perhaps throw in a little discount."

The company further engages in life cycle emails for members of its loyalty clubs, sending special messages with special offers for a member's birthday or anniversary, or even when the member's driver's license is about to expire.

"We send thank-you emails as well," Stoeppler says. "About a week after an Enterprise Plus member rents from us, they'll get a note thanking them for their business. It's the little touches like this that make a difference."

Email marketing is a powerful component within a full-spectrum marketing toolkit. There are many software programs that allow you to easily manage and send messages to your email lists for a very minimal cost. Many programs also provide rich analytics, allowing you to determine whether someone opened your email and clicked on any included links. More sophisticated software can even track a user's moves on the Web and tell you what pages they visited on your website. You can further determine how often certain customers do business with you, and even calculate how much each relationship is worth based on criteria you set.

Get the email address of every customer who does business with you, and start your own loyalty program, if it makes sense for your particular business. Also use email to drive customers back to both your website and social media outlets. Keep your messages short, interesting, and relevant, and don't send them out too often, unless your customers ask you to. For instance, I get several daily updates from one market research firm, all of which I find to be useful since they are helpful in my daily work. But being bombarded with specials every week from an online merchant that I only did business with once and feel no loyalty toward can quickly get annoying.

Email has become a very personal form of communication.

To me, it's a lot like a phone call. When someone sends an email to my personal address, it comes through either on my desktop or on my mobile device and gets my immediate attention. If it's something that's not relevant or wastes my time, it's akin to receiving an unsolicited phone call right as you sit down for dinner, and you know how that makes you feel.

Strategies for Effective Email Marketing

- Make your messages short and to the point.
- Use as few graphics as possible. (Lots of images scream spam. Emails with no images at all appear to be personal to the recipient and are therefore more likely to be read.)
- Send messages regularly, but with no more frequency than necessary.
- Automate your campaigns using one of the many available software providers.
- Measure your results, and modify your approach accordingly.
- Always include an easy way for customers to unsubscribe.

DON'T FORGET TO MARKET TO EMPLOYEES, TOO

It's true that many of these marketing channels are primarily geared toward reaching current and potential customers, but you should also endeavor to reach another very important constituency through your full-spectrum marketing efforts—your employees. The Enterprise brand does this in numerous ways, including through its TV ads, which speak to its workforce (and potential recruits) as much as to the public at large.

Within the marketing group, Enterprise has a whole team dedicated exclusively to communicating with the company's employees around the world. "The internal communications group sends out the same messages as everyone else in the marketing department, but they tweak it to reach our workforce," Farrell says. Messages are primarily disseminated through an internal website, known as the Hub. "I think of the Hub as our own social media site, where all of the messages are put in one place, and where employees can go to submit ideas and have a discussion," Farrell adds.

The company also has its own internal TV channel, called EHTV, for Enterprise Holdings Television. "When I first started at this company, I knew almost everybody," Andy Taylor says. "Today we have more than seventy thousand employees. Using tools like the Hub or EHTV allows us to let every one of those workers know that they are an important part of the company, wherever they live, and keeps them informed about what's happening on a regular basis."

The value of keeping employees updated about what's going on in the business cannot be overstated. Numerous studies show that a leading cause of employee disengagement is a feeling of not being plugged in to what's happening at the company. What's more, internal communications provide a way to publicly acknowledge individuals for their contributions to the company in a broader forum.

TELL YOUR STORY THROUGH THE MEDIA

Getting your business noticed through public relations and selective media placements should also be part of your full-spectrum marketing plan. "The discipline of PR is one of packaging your story in a truthful fashion in a way that's compelling enough to attract a reporter's interest because it's something people will want to hear," Farrell observes.

Start the process by figuring out which media outlets might be interested in telling your story. Today there are many options, from television stations to various online sites. Next, target your pitches so they are of relevance to the media outlet's audience. Reporters are always looking for a good story, but you must make sure what you're proposing is really going to be of broad interest. For example, if you're a Pilates instructor, it's highly unlikely the local health reporter will be interested in doing a profile on you, since there are countless other Pilates instructors in town who would like to be profiled as well. But maybe there is something unique about your background that might be of interest to readers. Perhaps you suffered from a debilitating illness that was cured through doing Pilates, and then you decided to become an instructor yourself to help others. That's an interesting human-interest angle. Or if a national study comes out showing the benefits of Pilates, you can offer to serve as an expert for your hometown paper, giving the story a local angle.

In dealing with the media, never stray from your message to convey the essence of what your brand is all about. You obviously can't give just marketing-related sound bites when a reporter interviews you, but you need to let your passion for your business, your customers, and your employees come through. When providing media coaching, I remind executives that a reporter can print only what you've actually said. So think through what quotes you would like to see appear in the article, and frame your responses to get those points across. It's what politicians do all the time. Have you noticed that candidates running for office never seem to answer the question they are asked, and instead reframe it to get their talking points in? If a politician is asked, "Why did you vote against that measure today?" you might hear them respond and reframe along the following lines: "The important point here is that we need to focus attention on how we're going to fight world hunger," or something to that effect.

"PR and marketing are both about storytelling," Farrell insists. "PR gives you more opportunity to tell a deeper, richer story than you can convey through advertising, but they work as a package. The message you put out from a PR perspective should reflect the message you're sending in your other marketing efforts."

MEASURE THE RETURN ON YOUR MARKETING INVESTMENT

Ultimately, you want to measure the effectiveness of your full-spectrum marketing efforts. What's the best way to do this?

"It's a very difficult question that companies struggle with, and it's the focus of intense debate in many boardrooms," Farrell observes. "For me, I look at a number of measures, starting with brand awareness. Through consumer research, we can measure how well people know and respect our brands, and that's something we monitor on a regular basis."

"We can also look at whether we are increasing our market share, doing more transactions, and growing the fleet," Stoeppler adds. "In addition, we use a brand tracker measurement to see what people think of the brand. Are they aware of our ads? Do they know our brand promise?"

If you have a loyalty program, you can measure the engagement of your most frequent customers. "We have six million Enterprise Plus members and we know that two and a half million of them rented with us last year," Stoeppler says. "We have a group within marketing communications that is focused solely on data analytics, so we have a tremendous amount of reporting and analysis that goes into what we do. It's a combination of the hard stuff, the analytics, combined with the softer stuff like brand health measurements."

When all of this is working together, you'll be able to more effectively gauge whether your full-spectrum marketing efforts are serving to effectively grow the business and instill loyalty, and you'll also be able to pinpoint which areas are in need of refinement.

KEYS TO DRIVING LOYALTY BY PRACTICING FULL-SPECTRUM MARKETING

1. Take advantage of the many marketing and communications channels at your disposal to get your message out and build a connection with your customers.
2. View marketing as good storytelling that involves using a variety of means to communicate a cohesive message about your brand.
3. Choose the right marketing channels for your business based on which media resonate best with your target audience.
4. Use social media to engage in a two-way dialogue with your customers by building a presence on sites such as Facebook, LinkedIn, and Twitter.
5. Make certain your website is easy to navigate, is informative, and provides a simple way for customers to reach you.
6. Promote your website through all of your marketing activities, and consider using QR codes to make it easy for smartphone users to get to your site.
7. When it comes to gathering fans or likes in the world of social media, focus on ***quality*** rather than ***quantity***.
8. Monitor what people are saying about your company on the various social media sites and immediately engage with those having an issue in order to get the matter resolved promptly offline.
9. Establish a loyalty program for your most frequent customers, and provide rewards that are relevant, of interest to your audience, and easy to redeem.
10. Try to get the email address for every customer—especially your most loyal ones—and stay in touch with them through regular communications.

11. Regulate the frequency of email messages based on customer preferences, and offer relevant information so that people look forward to opening and reading what you have to say.
12. Don't forget to also market to and regularly communicate with your employees, since feeling out of the loop about what's going on in the company is a leading cause of disengagement.
13. Use public relations to complement your other efforts, and always stay on message when conveying your story to the media.

9 Let Customers Fuel Your Growth

While growth is good—and something every company strives for—it must be carefully measured and centered on what's best for your customers and employees, not just your bottom line.

There are two primary ways to grow your business: organically (what is often described as "greenfield") or through acquisition. Businesses of all sizes primarily grow organically, by adding new products and services, entering new markets, or pursuing customers in different ways. Apple has done all three with huge success. It moved beyond just computers to offer iPhones, iPods, iPads, and an array of other products, allowing it to reach a whole new group of consumers around the world, and it began pursuing them through numerous channels, including a string of Apple retail stores.

As you gain scale and a strong balance sheet, acquisitions can be another way to buy growth faster than you could develop it on your own. Acquisitions work best when they allow you to quickly move into completely different areas, provide new opportunities for employees, and let you serve a broader group of customers than before. Sadly, research shows that the majority of corporate mergers and acquisitions are based largely on cost savings through synergies and other potential revenue drivers, which may explain why nearly three-quarters of them fail to deliver on initial expectations.

AVOID COMMON MERGER MISTAKES

While Enterprise's purchase of Vanguard Holdings proved to be a phenomenal success, the history of corporate acquisitions is riddled with failures: AOL and Time Warner, Quaker Oats and Snapple, MCI and WorldCom, and Daimler and Chrysler, just to name a few. A study by one research group looking at merger and acquisition deals over the past two decades found that in the vast majority of transactions, both companies involved would have been financially better off staying solo.

Why do mergers and acquisitions fail so often? Each case is slightly different, but there tend to be a number of common characteristics:

1. **An overreliance on consultants and public opinion.** Given the high odds of failure, many companies assume they need outside help to integrate an acquisition, and therefore often bring in consultants to help in the process. While consultants can play an important role, the advice they provide tends to be based on shorter-term trends. It's also common for outside consultants to be very smart but not necessarily knowledgeable about any particular industry. Enterprise did use consultants to assist with the Vanguard purchase, but primarily to help facilitate discussions among leaders in the organization about who would be responsible for making the acquisition work. "We have a strong institutional prejudice against consultants," admits Enterprise chief administrative officer Lee Kaplan. "Once they get in, they've got to be really good, because they are always just about to be fired." Why bring in consultants at all? Largely because you often don't know what you don't know. Consultants can come to the table with ideas you never thought of before. They can also help to create a structured process to follow when making decisions. "We designed our consultant relationship with a lot of off-ramps

along the way," Kaplan offers. "We probably got off on about the second off-ramp, which was more or less closing day." By then, Enterprise had developed a pretty good road map for the integration and didn't really need the outside help anymore. "We hired them largely to give us a process, but we made all of the important decisions," president and chief operating officer Pam Nicholson adds.

2. Making the merger all about synergies. A good acquisition always brings powerful synergies, but it needs to be about more than just cost savings and getting rid of a competitor. "Our purpose in the Vanguard acquisition was clearly growth," Kaplan says. "When you're doing it for growth, the motivation is dramatically different and the potential for success rises significantly." Adding the two companies together was immediately accretive to earnings, and over time Enterprise was able to find a number of synergies that led to greater efficiencies and significant cost savings.

3. Beginning the integration without proper planning. Despite the very narrow timeline, Enterprise went through a meticulous due diligence process before making a deal in the first place and ultimately blending the two companies together. Effective integration takes vision, an effective strategy, and constant communication throughout all levels of the organization. And it may mean doing nothing at all for a period of time until you take the time to get to know what you've bought and figured out the employees you've inherited. Only then can you start to ingrain a cohesive culture.

4. Failure to get proper buy-in from key leaders. Melding an existing business in with your own is extremely difficult. Your management team will likely have to work around the clock for a time to ensure that everything comes together as planned. If you want their support and dedication, you need to win them over to the idea before the deal ever gets done. While Andy Taylor was the ultimate decision maker, before signing an agreement he made sure everyone on his executive team not only had a chance to provide feedback but also was behind the idea 100 percent.

5. **Trying to merge equals.** What type of merger seems to have the highest failure rate? Those where two companies of the same size get together to form one huge behemoth. That's especially true when both businesses have similar services and an overlapping customer base. By contrast, when a larger successful corporation takes over a smaller business that brings with it new products, markets, and technologies, the odds of success multiply.

6. **Basing deals on ego and plans for transformational change.** The AOL–Time Warner merger is perhaps the biggest poster child for how to do everything wrong when buying another company. America Online merged with Time Warner in a deal valued at an eye-popping $350 billion back in 2000. It remains the largest—and by all accounts worst—merger in American business history. AOL co-founder Steve Case and Time Warner CEO Gerald Levin were convinced the Internet would transform all types of media. Case proclaimed the merger to be "a historic moment," while Levin said it would give customers unprecedented access to "every form of media" and unleash "immense economic growth." What it really led to was a string of job losses, a stock in free fall, and ultimately the breakup of both companies at a far lower valuation. The combined market capitalization of what remains of AOL and Time Warner today is a mere fraction of its value on the day of the merger. The biggest loser of all was Ted Turner, the largest individual shareholder in the combined company. He has been quoted as saying he lost 80 percent of his net worth, not to mention his job, for a total personal loss of around $8 billion.

7. **Buying due to fear and desperation.** Not to harp on the AOL–Time Warner debacle, but you could say that Case and Levin fell victim to the same belief that other CEOs of failed mergers have displayed: "If we don't make this deal—and make

it right now—we risk becoming irrelevant." Levin has said that he was trying to figure out how to transform Time Warner for the digital age when he met Case. Levin worried that his company might be left behind if he didn't do the AOL deal. But acting out of fear rarely makes sense, because it can often result in, among other things, our next point—overpaying for the purchase.

8. Overpaying. Andy Taylor likes to say that the best deal he ever made was the one he didn't. In terms of potential acquisition opportunities, the smart move most of the time is to pass, as Enterprise had done so many times before. Even though the company is more open to potential acquisitions now than at any moment in its history, the price has to be right. As just one example, Enterprise walked away from an opportunity to buy Advantage Rent-A-Car in 2009. At its peak, Advantage operated around 280 locations worldwide, before falling into bankruptcy. Enterprise offered $19 million to buy Advantage. When a bankruptcy judge decided to consider competing bids, Hertz stepped in with an offer of more than $30 million. Enterprise decided that was far too pricey and backed out. The company always runs financial projections and has a limit for what it is willing to pay. If the price is too high, it walks away. Incidentally, beyond price is the ability to pay for it. If the cost will put a severe strain on your balance sheet, even if it's a fair amount, it is probably not worth going forward with the deal.

CAPITALIZE ON ORGANIC OPPORTUNITIES

While Enterprise's experience in undertaking the acquisition of Alamo and National offers many lessons that can be applied to any business looking to expand, chances are in most cases your greatest opportunities for expansion will come organically. That is exactly how Enterprise grew from one location in 1957 to the global giant it was even before the acquisition in 2007. It's true that the company has become more aggressive about growth in recent years and is also willing to take more risks (albeit highly calculated to increase the odds of success). But in its early days, the exact opposite was true.

Jack Taylor was a great businessman, but he was fairly conservative. The company's drive for growth has largely come since Andy was appointed as president in 1980. On the day Andy took over, Enterprise had about fourteen thousand cars on lease and some five thousand rental vehicles, with revenues of less than $80 million and operations in about a dozen cities across four states. Andy and his senior team turned a good small business into a great one by using the principles instilled from an early age by his father. "I saw the power in our business model and really believed this could eventually become a global company," Andy Taylor recalls. "I've often joked that Jack and I are lucky that our birth order turned out the way it did. Jack didn't have the same kind of management skills I do, and I probably couldn't have taken the pay cut he did to start the company from scratch. He's a true entrepreneur, but managing a multibillion-dollar organization was never at the top of his list."

TAKE MEASURED RISKS

Under Jack's watch, Enterprise still experienced decent growth, but every move was carefully considered. Jack always began by calculating the potential loss he would suffer if things didn't work out as planned. "I wanted to know the downside risk and how much damage we would suffer if things turned out badly," Jack explains. He was even hesitant to sign long-term real estate leases, and thus was born the so-called JCT (Jack C. Taylor) Clause. The JCT Clause dates back to the 1970s, when the company began expanding into ever more markets. Jack wasn't sure Enterprise's midwestern approach would go over well in some of the larger, more crowded cities. When the manager of Enterprise's Florida operation wanted to open a branch in Fort Lauderdale, the owner of the property they had their eyes on wanted

$1,000 a month in rent and a five-year commitment. Jack liked the location but told the property owner he just couldn't agree to a lease that long, given his apprehension about whether things would work out. The two negotiated an addendum that came to be known as the JCT Clause. It allowed Enterprise to get out of its lease with ninety days' notice and payment of an additional ninety days' worth of rent. This language became part of the boilerplate for almost every lease the company negotiated, and it is among the ways risk was kept under control as Enterprise continued to grow into new areas.

DON'T EXPAND TOO QUICKLY

When things are going well, it's easy to let overconfidence lead to hasty expansion. Back in the early 1980s, Enterprise was growing revenues at more than 30 percent a year and opening new locations at a feverish pace. "We had many early successes, but unfortunately started to build too many branches, some in the wrong locations, and frankly we expanded faster than we could develop leaders," Andy Taylor admits. "We had a learning curve that I'm not sure we properly understood. For instance, we had to really figure out how to better manage our fleets in certain areas, since demand in many cities is quite seasonal. We lost a lot of money in the process of determining how to properly meet demand and position the fleet."

Expanding so fast also attracted the attention of some smaller competitors who started moving into Enterprise's home-city territory. They recognized how much success Enterprise was having and tried to replicate the model. The biggest difference was that most of the competitors attempted to grow quickly in order to go public or sell out. "We were a family-owned business focused on the long-term and taking care of our customers," Andy Taylor says. "A lot of these competitors ultimately went out of business or got acquired. I think the biggest takeaway for us from that time is that it's really all about taking a long-term view and being committed to success. And the way you get to that long-term view is through your people."

BE A NICHE PLAYER

Years ago, I led the marketing communications team at an investment firm that specialized in working with physicians and dentists. Granted, every money manager wants doctors as clients, since the perception is they make a lot of money and must have plenty to invest. Indeed, my aunt is a dentist and gets several cold calls a day from advisors hoping to earn her business. But what made our firm different was we truly did specialize in these professions, and our planning team understood what it took to run a successful medical or dental practice. As a result, in addition to investing a client's portfolio, we could offer proven strategies to help improve cash flows, bring in new patients, and so forth, all of which led to our clients having more money to spend and invest with us.

Because we built such a strong reputation for serving these niches so well through our marketing and branding efforts, we were able to form alliances with medical and dental associations around the country, allowing us to tap into their membership lists for direct mail campaigns. We also spoke at industry conventions, contributed articles to journals, and received a constant stream of referral business. Again, every investment firm wants to serve doctors, but we became the go-to company that this demographic believed was best positioned to serve its financial needs.

Were our investment results better than the competition's? Some years yes, others no. But doctors came to us because they trusted our expertise and believed our advice would make them more successful. At the end of the day, it wasn't simply about investment performance and whether we beat a given benchmark. We did everything we could to provide an excellent client experience for doctors, including creating an array of educational and practice management materials. As a result, the firm grew into one of the largest independent financial planning and investment management firms in the nation, and nearly 80 percent of its clients had something to do with the medical or dental profession.

I bring up this story to demonstrate the power of specialization and focusing on certain niches. That's exactly what Enterprise has done, starting with leasing and expanding into home-city car rentals. Specialization in the vehicle replacement market allowed Enterprise to own this space. Through Alamo and National, it now leads the market for airport rentals as well. And Enterprise Rent-A-Car expanded its commercial truck rental business in recent years by offering the same service to retail customers moving their homes.

The point is that you need not target only one narrow niche, especially if you have a number of different brands or lines of business. You just need to serve every chosen niche well. Since it's impossible for any one company to be all things to all people, having several brands under one umbrella has given Enterprise a huge advantage. It's an idea that just might be worth considering for your business.

LISTEN TO YOUR CUSTOMERS

The best way to determine where the hockey puck is headed, and therefore where you should be directing your company's future growth, often comes from talking directly to your customers. "If you ask, they will absolutely tell you what they are looking for," Nicholson insists. "We speak to our customers all the time, whether it's our insurance partners or corporate accounts. We also increasingly talk to our retail customers through our social media outlets. We want to know what they are seeing out there, and they aren't shy about letting us know what services they expect from us."

It's also critical to keep an eye on what's happening in the industry at large. After observing the ongoing interest in car sharing and a demand by consumers to be able to rent vehicles around the clock, the company started its Enterprise CarShare service and ultimately bought PhillyCarShare to better understand this retail business as it determines whether this is yet another niche with long-term potential.

CONSIDER FRANCHISING

In purchasing Vanguard, Enterprise inherited something it never expected to have before—franchisees. As part of their storied past, Alamo and National had taken on 120 franchise locations, and these came with the acquisition. Though this was initially viewed as a potential negative, Enterprise has come to view franchisees in a much different light and in fact now has a number of its own in Central and South America, as well as in Mexico. The company is currently looking into the possibility of adding even more franchises as an option for further fueling global growth.

Expanding your business to new geographic locations can be costly and time consuming. Franchising allows you to take a proven concept and replicate it by selling the rights to independent investors who use your name, products, and method of operation but are responsible for the cost of getting the business up and running. In essence, you license the right to operate under your name, and a local owner pays up-front and ongoing fees to use your brand, marketing materials, and operating techniques. The franchisees (or licensees) must adhere to your standards as part of the contract, but they are responsible for hiring and running these locations.

Wondering how well franchising works? Just look at McDonald's, 7-Eleven, Subway, Ace Hardware, Circle K, RE/MAX, Dunkin' Donuts, H&R Block, Snap-On Tools, Jiffy Lube, Curves, SuperCuts, Roto-Rooter, Jani-King, and Marriott Hotels, all of which have grown into giants in their respective industries as a direct result of franchising.

Keep in mind that franchising has its pitfalls. For one thing, building a cohesive culture becomes more challenging. But it's one way to grow organically that can be effective, depending on your business and whether it lends itself to such an option.

THINK GLOBAL

In today's world it's important to consider your options for growth outside of your home country. "Enterprise always wanted to become a global brand, which is why we entered Canada and then expanded into the United Kingdom, Ireland, and Germany," Nicholson says. Enterprise made its first foray outside the United States by expanding to Canada in the early 1990s, and it has operated in Europe since 1994.

While overseas expansion offers significant possibilities, it also comes with cultural differences that must be respected. Enterprise learned some of these lessons the hard way. When it opened its first office in the United Kingdom, experts warned that Europeans didn't really care about customer service and that the company's merit-based system was unlikely to go over well with potential job candidates. As it turned out, neither was true, and Enterprise ultimately discovered that good customer service knows no boundaries and that lots of workers prefer to be compensated like entrepreneurs.

Nevertheless, the company found it more difficult to build its brand and deal with differing dynamics overseas. Among other things, there's not much of an insurance replacement business in the United Kingdom. Body shops typically have their own loaner vehicles and build the cost of using them into the overall repair price. Enterprise therefore had to structure its practices a bit differently and manage its European fleet accordingly. (The company learned that Germans like to rent and drive German cars, for instance. And while white is the most popular color in America, customers in the United Kingdom prefer silver.) Though the company lost money during its initial learning phase, Enterprise's operation in Europe is now highly profitable.

Beyond Ireland, Germany, the United Kingdom, and Canada, international expansion took a backseat following the

Vanguard acquisition, which closed less than a year before the global economic downturn began. After successfully integrating Alamo and National and dealing with the recession, Enterprise has once again turned its attention overseas. Half of the worldwide rental car industry is in North America, and Enterprise already leads in that market. Another quarter is in Europe, and the remainder is in the rest of the world. Of that percentage, five countries make up the majority of all business in Europe: the United Kingdom, Germany, France, Spain, and Italy. "We made many trips to Europe and looked at every single company in each country, with a focus on France and Spain, given that we already had a presence in the United Kingdom, Germany, and Ireland," Nicholson says. "We realized that getting scale at airports and rail stations, which is where most cars in France and Spain are rented, would take years, since these locations are so hard to come by. We spotted a company that looked perfect for what we wanted to do, and luckily it was for sale."

Enterprise entered into an agreement with PSA Peugeot Citroën's French car rental subsidiary, Citer SA, and its Spanish subsidiary, Atesa, in late 2011. The deal closed in January 2012. Citer SA has deep coverage through locations in city centers, railway stations, and airports throughout France and Spain. "This acquisition has no overlap to our current operations in Europe and really was done in response to the needs of our customers who have been asking us to expand our footprint in Europe," Andy Taylor notes. With the acquisition, Enterprise is now the number three rental car company in Europe overall, ranking first in the United Kingdom and fourth in both Spain and France. "Importantly, being global sends a powerful message to our employees," Ross points out. "They can really see the opportunities available to them as the company grows. It also makes them feel good to know they are part of an expanding business. After we announced the Citer transaction, I attended a dinner with a group of employees who will probably never work in France or Spain, yet they felt excited to be part of a company that was gaining an expanded global presence."

PREPARE FOR TOUGH TIMES BEFORE THEY ARRIVE

While we all would like to see growth continue on an uninterrupted upward trajectory, that's not how things happen in the real world. As a result, any smart growth strategy also calls for being prepared for the tough times that will eventually come no matter how well you manage your business. Perhaps the most devastating time in recent memory was the financial crisis of 2008, which hit almost every company around the world hard.

The sudden economic slowdown took most people by surprise and was far-reaching. Credit markets froze, the stock market plunged, unemployment jumped, and consumers stopped spending on anything but the essentials.

The car rental industry got whacked from all sides. People weren't traveling or renting vehicles, which hurt business. At the same time, auto companies struggled like never before, with General Motors filing for bankruptcy and ultimately being bailed out by the U.S. government.

Enterprise suffered a chain reaction of events during this time. By September 2008, the situation was looking increasingly severe. Travel slowed down, and people were renting fewer cars. At the same time, the used car market was essentially dead, and vehicles Enterprise had ordered before the recession hit were starting to arrive along with bills for payment. This chain reaction began to impact the company's balance sheet.

To deal with the situation, Andy and a team of about fifteen senior Enterprise managers began to meet every morning at eight to figure out how they would navigate their way through this extremely difficult period. How much money was in the bank? Were their business partners still functioning? What else could possibly go wrong? "We were in the midst of a really dark period," Andy admits. "We faced a series of terrible options. It was by far the most difficult period I have ever been through in this business. The only thing even comparable was during the 1974 energy crisis, when we had a lot full of gas guzzlers that weren't selling. My father was basically checking the cash box every night to see if we had anything left. I was worried sick, but he was gutsy and cool, calming us down and offering assurance that eventually things would return to normal."

Andy remembered that admonition from his dad now that he was in charge and responsible for being a calming influence on the rest of the team, including his daughter and niece, who hold executive roles in the company and had never been through a challenging period of this nature before. "I told everyone in our 'situation room' one day that if we lost $150 million it would be okay," he shares. "I just didn't want to lose ten times that amount. We had to make some tough decisions to right the business, but it made us a far better company in the end." The hardest part was deciding to reduce head count for the first time in Enterprise history, by 4.5 percent, while dropping the overall fleet size by 10 percent. "It was so unnatural for us to do this, and I think it came as a shock to our people," he says. "But we all got on the same page pretty quickly as we saw the urgency of the matter."

Enterprise wound up losing money for nearly three months in a row, though it never had a down fiscal quarter, even during the toughest times. All told, the company cut more than $370 million from annual expenses. Employees were asked to sacrifice as well. The company put a freeze on raises, reduced overtime, slashed business travel, and curtailed any training programs that weren't considered essential. As challenging as it was, Enterprise made adjustments that were far less difficult than those made by many other companies.

As the months progressed and the economy slowly recovered, these "situation room" meetings ultimately moved to twice a week and then once a week before occurring on an as-needed basis. Andy compares the recession of 2008–9 to football camp: you are better and stronger for having gone through it, but you never want to relive the experience again. "Acting quickly and decisively was hard, but it put our company and our employees in a much stronger position to take advantage of emerging opportunities as the economy began to recover," he says.

At the end of the day, Enterprise came out on the other side with a better understanding of how to effectively run and grow your business in the good times, while always being ready for the unexpected. These lessons include:

1. Distinguish between the necessary and the nice-to-haves. Enterprise once held grand annual meetings for its branch managers, with splashy arena-sized programs, including guest speakers and a full concert by a popular band for more than seven thousand attendees. The events, held in Orlando, were paid for by the company, including everything from airfare and hotels to meals and entertainment. When the economy turned, Enterprise severely limited the number of people eligible to attend this event, to less than one thousand. The company also cut back on travel and meetings across the organization, to keep these expenses to a minimum. Executives even required that copies be double-sided and paper clips be recycled, since every penny counted. Now that the economy has improved, it would be easy for costs to creep back in, but the company continues to think with the same mind-set it put into place back in 2008. "We've literally taken hundreds of millions of dollars of cost a year out of the business," Andy shares. "It's a total change in mind-set, and we can't afford to return to what we had before."

2. Don't be a prisoner of hope. It's easy to grow complacent, or even stuck in place, when faced with a difficult situation. Your tendency is to put your hands up, hope for the best, and pray that the storm passes quickly. But in challenging economic times, every day counts. Inaction is the enemy. Lenders must be willing to trust you to make the hard choices to keep your business afloat. Some of these decisions can be very tough, especially when they involve people's lives. But failure to act can put your company's very existence in jeopardy.

3. Communicate, communicate, communicate. In difficult periods, everyone can feel the tension, including your employees. Even if they have no idea how your balance sheet looks, they can sense when things aren't going well. During what proved to be a very challenging time financially, Enterprise, as in the past, was completely honest with everyone. Andy continually sent out messages to the entire workforce, from memos to recorded videos, letting them know exactly what was happening. "I went to the family and said, 'We're not taking any money out of the business right now until we get through this period,' and I made sure to tell our people that," he says. "I wanted them to know we were in this with them and we'd get past this difficult time together."

4. Understand the difference between real partners and transactional friends. They say that during the toughest times you learn whom you can really count on, and that's true in business as well. Enterprise has been built largely on long-term partnerships, from travel suppliers and insurance companies to auto manufacturers and financial institutions (as you'll discover in the next chapter). During the economic downturn, Andy says it became really clear who the company's true partners were. At the same time, Enterprise stood by even the most financially troubled carmakers, honoring payments for vehicles even when doing so put a strain on the company's balance sheet. "I think they really admired us for that, and when you treat your partners well, they will return the favor to you," Andy observes.

5. Continue to take good care of your customers. When you're trying to save money, it's tempting to scrimp on some of the niceties that help to enhance the customer experience. But, just like your business partners, customers will remember how they were treated in more challenging environments. In a bad economy, everyone is hurting. The more you can do to let customers know how much you value their business, and the less you take away when the going gets tough, the more loyalty you'll build for when you turn the corner. The goodwill you can earn from taking care of customers—and employees—when they are hurting most is immeasurable.

KEYS TO DRIVING LOYALTY BY LETTING CUSTOMERS FUEL YOUR GROWTH

1. Consider buying growth if it is a strategic fit and allows you to offer new and different services to a broader target market, thus meeting a wider array of customer needs.
2. If you decide to grow through acquisition, avoid overpaying, regardless of how badly you want to own the other company.
3. While you should always be focused on organic growth, it's important to be open to expanding in ways that might be outside of your comfort zone, especially when a unique opportunity comes along.
4. Ensure that everyone on your executive team supports any decision to enter into a merger or acquisition, and take your time integrating both companies (haste tends to magnify any integration challenges).
5. Take calculated risks, but don't enter into any situation that stands to be financially devastating if it works out badly.
6. Embrace the power of specialization and learn how to serve your primary niches better by talking directly with your customers.
7. If appropriate for your business, consider the potential of franchising as a way to expand geographically.
8. Explore options for expanding your business outside of your home country, especially given that we live in such a global world.
9. Be prepared for the tough times that will eventually come, in order to keep your company on solid ground during the most challenging periods.

10 Form Lifelong Partnerships

My friend Maxine Clark likes to say that, in business, you can make 1 + 1 = 10. Maxine is the founder and chief executive bear of Build-A-Bear Workshop, the popular retail chain that lets customers create and outfit their own customized stuffed animals. In coming up with this equation, she's not talking about partaking in some kind of financial shenanigan in order to further your interests. Rather, Maxine believes you can turn 1 + 1 into something very powerful by joining forces with a partner. "For most companies, one plus one only equals two," Maxine says. "That's because they choose to go slowly, taking small steps, rather than looking for huge-leap strategic synergies." The right partnership can help catapult you into a much greater success than you could ever become on your own.

Maxine lives this belief by example. Build-A-Bear Workshop has more than four hundred locations worldwide today, with annual net sales of around $400 million. But even back when the company had just a single location at the Saint Louis Galleria Mall in 1997, Maxine was already thinking big. As her company began to grow, she noticed that many customers walked in carrying bags from Limited Too. Wouldn't it be great, she thought, if she could carry a line of Limited Too clothes for customers to dress their stuffed bears in? Although Limited Too was significantly larger than Build-A-Bear, she decided to propose such a partnership. Limited Too ultimately agreed, and sales exceeded even her most optimistic expectations.

Maxine also turned 1 + 1 into 10 when she approached Major League Baseball about offering licensed uniforms for her bears. That proved to be another huge win and broadened out her customer base to attract more boys into the stores. She even turned that partnership into a way for Build-A-Bear to open stores at several major-league ballparks. This belief in the power of strategic alliances eventually led Maxine to partnerships with the National Basketball Association and National Football League, along with Disney, Warner Brothers, and Skechers footwear. "These partnerships give us exposure to audiences and markets we could never reach on our own, and vice versa," Maxine says. "In today's world, consumers are inundated with loud marketing messages practically everywhere they turn. As a result, to get through all this noise, your offering has to be really special. One way to accomplish this is by adding value through partnerships that create huge 'wow' experiences for your customers."

PARTNERING CAN LEAD TO EXPONENTIAL GROWTH

Two of your most important partners are your loyal customers and employees. Partnering with customers to meet their needs and solve their problems can certainly help both of you turn 1 + 1 into 10. At the same time, partnering with your employees is an essential ingredient to driving the business forward, which means empowering them to make decisions and allowing them to benefit from the company's success. Some of your best ideas for moving the company forward are bound to come from your employees, who are closest to the business and work directly with your customers every day. That's certainly been true at Enterprise, which has grown largely based on the ingenuity of its homegrown management team.

Enterprise's decision to let some of its managers form partnerships with outside organizations has arguably helped the company turn 1 + 1 into 1,000. The company has formed literally thousands of partnerships across all of its brands, and these relationships account for an overwhelming percentage of its overall business.

"Each one of our brands has a slightly different partnership customer base," says president and chief operating officer Pam Nicholson. "Enterprise has formed very close ties with insurance companies, body shops, car dealerships, and corporate accounts. National is very big on the corporate side. Alamo focuses largely on partnerships with tour companies, hotels, and airlines. In all cases, these partnerships are a very important part of our business."

What Enterprise has discovered is that you need to continually earn and cultivate the loyalty of your partners, since they have the potential to help build your business exponentially. You also must remember that such arrangements come with important responsibilities. When you partner with an organization, their customers become your customers. This means your employees have to represent both organizations well. Otherwise, it could put the partnership—and both of your brands—into jeopardy. Enterprise takes this duty very seriously, as demonstrated by how it handles business from one of its most important partners, insurance companies.

SAVE YOUR PARTNERS MONEY

If you get into an automobile accident anywhere in America today, there's a 90 percent chance that your insurance company will send you to Enterprise Rent-A-Car for a temporary replacement vehicle. Enterprise has contracts with all of the major auto insurers, which negotiate special rates and get billed directly for the cost of the rental, so policyholders don't have to worry about making payments. At the same time, Enterprise has similar partnerships with body shops and service stations. So even if you aren't working through your insurance provider, there's a high probability the shop will recommend you call Enterprise, taking advantage of the special rates they've worked out for their customers.

The idea for these partnerships came somewhat serendipitously. Back in the 1960s, while working at what essentially was the second Enterprise Rent-A-Car location in downtown St. Louis, employees Don Ross and Doug Brown were trying to figure out how to round up business for the ten cars in their fleet. While walking back to the office from lunch one day, they happened to pass by a building with a sign for AAA Missouri insurance. On a lark, Ross suggested they stop in to talk with the insurance adjuster, hoping to get some referrals. At the time, insurance companies didn't pay for car rentals. They instead gave policyholders money to either cover cab fare or help out with rental costs when vehicles were stolen or damaged in an accident. Brown thought they should pitch the idea of just having the insurance company cover the rental instead of handing over cash, especially if that wound up being cheaper.

The adjuster was intrigued by Brown's pitch, which was to provide cars to policyholders for $5 a day and 5 cents per mile. The price went over well, although the adjuster said he had no interest in paying 5 cents a mile, since that could increase the cost substantially. So Brown and Ross dropped the mileage charge, with the agreement that the insurance company pay for the rental directly.

This wound up being an experiment that has paid huge dividends for Enterprise. Without realizing it, Brown and Ross tapped into a huge pool of potential renters, and a market segment that ultimately led Enterprise to become the largest car rental company in North America. As the company continued to build partnerships with other insurance companies, it quickly came to lead the home-city market, renting to local residents in need of temporary transportation due to an accident or repair, or to accommodate some other need.

Enterprise has cultivated relationships with thousands of business partners, including insurers, auto manufacturers, tour companies, corporations, car dealerships, body shops, and even credit unions. These partnerships give the company a huge competitive advantage. What's impressive is how far Enterprise will go to make sure these partnerships are win-win for both sides.

KEEP ALL SIDES INFORMED

As Enterprise grew its insurance partnerships, branch managers started to do more to strengthen these relationships and build additional trust. Among other things, Enterprise employees offered to monitor a policyholder's entire repair process. This was important because both the insurance companies and the end customer were in a hurry to get out of the rental as soon as possible.

Renting a replacement vehicle can be complicated. Since no one plans on having an accident, you often need the car quickly and sometimes may not understand how long your insurance company will provide coverage. In addition, the length of the rental is always changing, since you're dependent on the time it takes to get the repairs done. While you can obtain an up-front estimate, the actual time could be longer before repairs are made to your complete satisfaction.

To keep all sides in the loop, Enterprise started following up with body shops on a daily basis, to let insurance partners know how the repairs were coming along. This also helped Enterprise employees to better manage the fleet, allowing them to identify in advance which customers would likely need to keep their vehicles out longer. When informing adjusters about the status, they could get approval to extend the rental as necessary. It was a pretty laborious process, but Enterprise felt the extra service provided was worth it.

For many years this was a manual effort, right down to the final billing. Enterprise employees kept rental agreements in accordion files marked A, B, and C. A files were for the insurance companies, B files had records for the body and repair shops, and C files contained information on the renters. Tracking repair times required many back-and-forth phone calls, since almost nothing was automated. From the initial call that a car was needed to the frequent check-ins with repair shops, each rental easily required a dozen or more calls. By the early 1990s, as the number of insurance rentals skyrocketed, telephone traffic across all branches was estimated at six hundred thousand calls a day.

DO THE RIGHT THING, EVEN IF IT COSTS YOU MORE MONEY

Though insurance partners were appreciative of these efforts, they wanted to cut down on all of the back-and-forth phone calls and faxes. In 1994, several insurers asked Enterprise to find a better solution. In response, Enterprise tapped three executives to figure out how to make the rental process for insurance customers more seamless all the way around.

The team gathered together claims adjusters and information services personnel from various companies and held brainstorming sessions. Enterprise did the same with its own internal team, comprised of employees who worked most closely on insurance rentals. In all cases they charted the rental process from accident to repair completion to the ultimate return of the vehicle. Enterprise employees then traveled around the country visiting the offices of a major insurance company partner to get an up-close look at how the process worked from the customer's perspective.

While visiting one insurer's claims center, Enterprise employees were stunned by the sheer volume of calls going to and coming from Enterprise Rent-A-Car branches. Adjusters talked about how these conversations could monopolize their entire day. Nearly all of the calls had to do with getting permission to extend rentals. Enterprise realized it needed to find a way to automate this task, but that was a complicated assignment. Integrating systems is never easy, but it was made even tougher by the diversity of hardware that each insurance company used.

Enterprise ultimately mapped out a solution that was flexible enough to work for everyone. The system has come to be known as ARMS, short for Automated Rental Management System. The earliest version was designed to let insurance companies manage the entire rental process with Enterprise electronically, linking their mainframes to Enterprise's IBM AS/400 microcomputers. Later iterations added to this experience by providing access through the Internet and automatically tracking the vehicle repair process, allowing dealers and body shops to enter status updates into the system, taking away the need for phone calls. This created far greater efficiencies and freed up considerable bandwidth for everyone.

With ARMS, when a policyholder gets into an accident, the insurance adjuster simply logs on and creates a reservation. This gets electronically submitted to the nearest Enterprise branch office, based on the customer's phone number or zip code. Once the reservation is received, an Enterprise employee contacts the customer to set up the rental details, and then monitors the whole process online. That way, adjusters can better understand what's going on with the repairs and see how long the car will be out.

It's important to note that Enterprise green-lighted the development of ARMS without doing a cost analysis. "It was something we knew had to be done," Andy Taylor explains. "It was the right thing for our customers, for our insurance partners, and for our employees." The ultimate price tag for ARMS was around $40 million.

While it might seem counterintuitive, one of Enterprise's goals in building ARMS was to *reduce* the number of days cars are rented by insurance companies by making the process more efficient. Why would Enterprise want to do something like this, since the company makes more money the more frequently and longer a car is out? Some Enterprise branch managers wondered the same thing. In 2000, as ARMS was coming into full implementation, the average replacement rental was fourteen days. By the company's calculations, occupancy of the Enterprise fleet might fall 4 percent for each rental day eliminated through these efficiencies.

But the Enterprise team realized that those worried this would stall growth weren't thinking about it the right way. As Andy pointed out, if done correctly, ARMS would actually lead to *more* business. Given the benefits it offered, it indeed attracted additional business, and Enterprise's insurance partners became even more loyal.

"The decision to build ARMS was a slam dunk, because if you understand our culture and what we're all about, it comes down to doing the right thing for our company by doing the right thing for our customers and our business partners," Andy says.

DOCUMENT YOUR RELATIONSHIP IN WRITING

Enterprise solidifies its insurance partner relationships through what are referred to as preferred provider option arrangements, or PPOs. These agreements outline what services Enterprise will perform for the insurance companies, and in turn ask them to give Enterprise a larger share of rentals in exchange for using the ARMS technology and competitive pricing. At one point the two sides spent most of the time dickering over the daily rental price when putting together a new PPO, but that became less of an issue once the insurance companies realized they would save more money using ARMS than by getting a cheaper rate from another competitor.

"We showed them that if you lower the rate by $1, on a fourteen-day rental you'll only save $14," Ross says. "But if we could help them cut back on the length of the rental through our in-depth management and reporting process, taking it from fourteen to twelve days, they would save significantly more."

That's exactly what happened. The average rental length for insurance replacements has dropped by an average of two days since ARMS was fully launched. Despite the savings for insurance partners, Enterprise's fleet has continued to grow, allaying the fears of those initially skeptical managers.

"The reason we've grown so much and earned more business is because we've built the most cost-effective and best infrastructure for our insurance partners," Ross insists. "Plus, we offer excellent customer support and can deliver a scope of services that our insurance partners were never exposed to before. They are often amazed at the lengths our branches will go to in order to please them."

One insurance partner told me that Enterprise was the first car rental company to understand that getting a higher number of transactions automated would save—and therefore make—everyone more money. The ARMS system also automates payment processing, saving insurance companies from ever having to cut a check, and eliminating the need for Enterprise to mail out what used to be six million invoices a year. There are rarely any billing disputes now, since comprehensive tracking notes for every rental can be found inside the ARMS records.

Enterprise spends some $10 million a year on upgrades to ARMS and related applications, which are used by more than three hundred insurance companies, seven thousand body shops, and thousands of car dealers around the world.

Another value proposition Enterprise offers is the excellent customer service provided by its employees. When an insurance company, body shop, or car dealership refers business to Enterprise, the Enterprise employee acts as a de facto representative of the partner as well. If a policyholder has a good experience with the car rental process, they'll think the insurance company did a good job taking care of them, even though the service was really provided by Enterprise. The Enterprise employees at every branch office understand that and are trained to go the extra mile to represent partner companies. When picking you up from the body shop, Enterprise workers will likely reassure you that you've selected a good place to have your vehicle fixed. They'll also talk about your insurance company by name and explain the whole process, including what's covered.

"In this capacity, we really are an extension of the insurer or other service provider," Andy Taylor says. "We want to tell the insured or claimant, 'Our experience is that your insurance company does a great job of settling claims, and I'm sure that is not going to be an issue for you. Our main concern is getting you into an appropriate car that will satisfy your needs, and we'll do it fast so you can get back to work or wherever you need to go.' We then follow through on the whole process, making sure both Enterprise and the insurance company do a good job of taking care of the customer."

Enterprise, through ARMS, is also the touch point customers can call to find out how the repairs are coming along, whether the insurance company will allow them to keep the rental longer than initially promised, and so forth. How employees treat customers through every moment of truth in the Cycle of Service reflects on many different parties.

"If our local managers deliver great service to the customers of our partners during a time of need, everyone wins," Nicholson says.

Benefits of Forming Successful Partnerships

1. Get access to a much larger potential customer base.
2. Improve weaknesses by tapping into your partner's strengths.
3. Provide a broader range of products and services.
4. Leverage your partner's brand name.
5. Look bigger than you are.
6. Turn your partner's loyal customers into your loyal customers.

PARTNER WITH YOUR SUPPLIERS

Enterprise has further formed strong partnerships with the auto manufacturers that supply its vehicles. The company has PPO agreements with several carmakers and is one of the largest customers of General Motors, Ford, and Chrysler.

"It's important to have relationships with many carmakers, since we purchase more than six hundred thousand vehicles each year in the United States alone," Nicholson says. "We need a variety of models to make sure we're getting the highest residual value when it comes time to remarket these vehicles." Enterprise buys an estimated 3 to 5 percent of all vehicles manufactured in the United States annually, making it one of the largest private purchasers of new cars in the world.

"There's definitely some negotiation involved in making sure we get the best transaction possible, but we assure them that we're amicable partners in the end," Nicholson says. "We find ways to come to an agreement based on their needs, what works for us, and taking into account any current and expected future incentives."

Enterprise takes its partnership with carmakers a step further by having the vehicles delivered and sold from independently owned dealerships near each branch. This supports businesses in the community, keeps tax dollars local, and helps to strengthen relationships with the dealers, many of which are also partners that house on-site Enterprise branches and refer business to the company when customers have cars in for service.

Once it comes time to remarket these vehicles, Enterprise often sells them back to the dealers they were purchased from for their used car lots. "Some dealers will call and say, 'I need ten of this model in this particular color with this amount of mileage,' and we'll go through our fleet to find these vehicles," Nicholson says. "The dealers know that if one of the cars shows up on the lot with a scratch or dent or something we didn't describe, we'll take it back and get them something else."

CONSTANTLY BE ON THE LOOKOUT FOR POTENTIAL SYNERGIES

The success of Enterprise's own retail car sales division is due in large part to partnerships it has formed over the years with various credit unions. Customer referrals from member credit unions account for about 30 percent of all such transactions. These partnerships go back to 1985. Up to that point, Enterprise sold its used cars the old-fashioned way: by advertising in local papers. Although its no-haggle policy set it apart, it essentially looked like every other car seller in town.

"We came up with an idea to approach the Missouri Credit Union League in St. Louis about staging a one-day car sales event just for its members," Ross recalls. "That first special sale proved to be successful. We immediately realized how valuable credit union partnerships were and soon held more one-day events around the country."

It's a logical partnership that benefits both sides. The credit unions make money on the car loans members take out to purchase the vehicles, while Enterprise enjoys access to a captive audience of buyers. "The arrangement is particularly attractive to credit unions because 40 percent of all loans they grant are for automobiles," Ross explains. "When members go buy a car on their own, without being part of a referral program like this, they often finance through the dealership instead. We make sure all of our sales keep the financing with the credit union that sent us the business. In addition, the members get to take advantage of our 100 percent guarantee, which puts the credit unions at ease knowing the transaction will be a smooth one."

Credit union members can also buy vehicles from Enterprise on the Web through a co-branded Enterprise Car Sales site. Members are able to sort available vehicles by year, make, model, price, mileage, color, and location. The technology gives members a detailed review of the vehicle, including photos, features, and colors. Members can even get approved for financing online, and Enterprise guarantees that the credit union sending the customer to the website gets 100 percent of all car loans resulting from any purchases.

LOYALTY BEGETS LOYALTY

Enterprise has also established a number of other partnerships across its various brands. Alamo has developed a niche in working with different airlines and other travel providers, becoming the number one car rental company for international visitors to North America. The company has a very close relationship with Disney and serves as the official rental car company of the Walt Disney World Resort in Florida, Disneyland Resort in California, and Disney's Aulani Resort on the Hawaiian island of Oahu.

National has agreements with hundreds of corporations to provide special rates and other employee perks, and it is the official car rental company of organizations such as the PGA of America.

Enterprise even formed a partnership with IKEA in Belfast, Northern Island, to provide hourly van rentals for customers needing to take home large items that won't fit in their own vehicles. This arrangement has since been expanded to other countries, and follows on the heels of a similar arrangement that Enterprise struck with Walmart.

If done right, you can turn the loyal customers of your partners into loyal customers of your own business. There are no doubt countless boys who would have never walked into a Build-A-Bear Workshop store had Maxine Clark not formed a partnership with the National Football League. After coming in to get a bear adorned in 49ers gear, for instance, a decent number of these young male fans return for other items, including gifts for the girlfriends, daughters, and sisters in their lives.

Enterprise knows that if those customers experiencing the company's services through an insurance referral are impressed, they'll also come back the next time they need a replacement car or go on vacation. Such positive customer relationships can become a virtuous circle that helps to power your business forward in good times and bad.

FIVE RULES FOR FORMING SUCCESSFUL BUSINESS PARTNERSHIPS

Enterprise essentially follows five core principles when establishing partnerships, which nearly any business can use to make 1 + 1 = 10, if not considerably more.

1. Solve your partner's problems. When Enterprise had a single brand, the company realized it was unable to meet the needs of many corporate customers. "They could do business with us in the home city, but they told us we fell short at offering service at the airport and in other countries around the world," Nicholson shares. "As we looked to fill this gap, we realized one way to do it was through acquisition. That's a key reason we bought Alamo and National, and why we've also purchased some international car rental companies. We're now in a position to effectively provide what our partners want and expect from us."

Likewise, when building ARMS, Enterprise went out to its insurance company partners to see what type of system would be of the greatest benefit to them. "They said, 'We need to reduce our total cost per transaction and we're having a hard time managing the repair shops,'" Ross explains. "We listened to their problems and came up with a solution. We didn't think about the cost of doing this. We just did it." Enterprise even took a slight initial hit to its revenues, since ARMS helped insurers to cut the number of rental days. But the system engendered incredible loyalty, resulting in significant new business from its happy and grateful insurance partners.

2. Make the relationship mutually rewarding. At the end of the day, any partnership arrangement needs to be a win for both sides. "You can't just do everything you or your partner wants, because that would make the deal purely one-sided," Nicholson explains. "You've got to identify what you both need and say, 'I'll do this for you, but here's what I need in return.' It's the classic win-win situation. If you're both winning, then you have a true partnership."

3. Don't go for the last oink out of the pig. It's natural for two parties to walk into partnership negotiations focused on how each can come away with the best terms possible. In some cases, people try to wring out every last penny to their advantage. Enterprise certainly wants to come away with a favorable arrangement, but it is more concerned about building a strong relationship that can endure for the next ten years, not just ten months. "I like to tell our people that it's not about getting the last oink out of the pig," says Andy Taylor. "This doesn't mean we don't negotiate hard, or that we never have issues with our partners. But we try to always work together, even in areas where we disagree, toward a common goal."

4. Collaborate and keep the lines of communication open. One reason Enterprise's many partnerships work so well is because there is constant back-and-forth between the two sides in an effort to improve the overall customer experience. Staying in regular communication will give you a better sense of what your partners need, and in turn provide a better understanding of how you can be of more help to each other.

"We always have our eye on where the hockey puck is going to be," Andy Taylor says. "We ask questions like: 'How can we add more value for you? How can we help your business? What more can we provide to make your business easier?' "

5. Never rest on your laurels. Even after a partnership is in place, you have to keep re-earning the trust of your partners all the time. "At the end of the day, even with the PPO agreements in place, nothing would stop any one of our customers from kicking us out the door if we weren't providing the right kind of service and taking care of their needs," Ross admits.

Other rental car companies are always out there looking to steal away business from Enterprise's partners. If the company doesn't stay on its toes by continuing to exceed customer expectations, that business may land in the hands of someone else that will.

"We are always trying to get better and do more for our partners," Nicholson adds. "We are continually learning from them as well about how to make innovations in our own business, which benefits everyone."

KEYS TO DRIVING LOYALTY BY FORMING LIFELONG PARTNERSHIPS

1. Look to form alliances with other companies and organizations that can help your business turn 1 + 1 into 10.
2. Partner with customers to meet their needs and solve their problems in ways they might not have thought of before.
3. Partner with employees as well, since they can provide some of the best ideas for helping to move your business forward.
4. Identify other companies you can join forces with and continually work to earn and cultivate their loyalty.
5. Find creative ways to approach potential partners, and always demonstrate the potential benefits from both sides.
6. Do what's necessary to ensure the long-term success of your partners.
7. Solidify your partnership arrangements in writing, outlining what both sides bring to the table and confirming your mutual commitments to each other.
8. To form a win-win arrangement, look to solve your partner's problems, make the relationship mutually rewarding, don't try to wring out every last penny to your advantage, keep the lines of communication open, and never rest on your laurels.

11 Build a Sustainable Business

Not long ago, the ultimate measure of a company's success was based almost exclusively on the bottom line. A strong balance sheet, healthy revenues, and, in the case of publicly traded organizations, stellar stock market performance were among the primary yardsticks by which corporations were judged. Oftentimes the means of generating revenues didn't matter, as long as they continued to rise.

Over time, it became clear that this drive for profits above all came at a steep price. History is rife with examples of companies that pushed too far to make the numbers with little regard for how such actions would affect people and the planet. For instance, juries have found tobacco companies guilty of covering up evidence about the huge health risks posed by smoking, in order to sell more cigarettes. Oil companies once pillaged land and obliterated natural resources with zealous drilling. Apparel companies have been known to exploit workers in overseas sweatshops as a way of lowering costs. And the list goes on.

Thankfully, the business world has begun to think much differently in recent years, forming more of a nexus between financial performance and operations conducted in an environmentally friendly manner. This focus has come to be known as the "triple bottom line," which gives equal weight to economic, environmental, and social performance. The term *sustainabil-*

ity is often used synonymously with *triple bottom line* because companies view this three-pronged approach as essential to the continued existence of our communities, our environment, and their businesses. Sustainable corporations earn an honest profit by treating their employees, customers, and others fairly and with dignity, while at the same time protecting the environment.

Enterprise has long thought about issues related to sustainability but began to make it a more formalized part of its business in 2007. A year later the company appointed a head of sustainability and started to take a closer look at how it could become a better corporate citizen. "While having an official process around sustainability is a relatively new idea for us, the principles of the triple bottom line have really been a part of our culture since this company's founding," observes Lee Broughton, Enterprise's head of corporate identity and sustainability. "Jack Taylor's concept of taking care of your customers and employees first and letting the profits follow is a primary example of sustainability. In many respects, the fact that this is a privately held, family-run organization in itself is a very sustainable concept. So we really started thinking about this concept of the triple bottom line long before it became more formalized."

Focusing attention on the combination of people, planet, and profits not only is the right thing to do, it also has the potential to be a powerful positive force for you and your business. What once was referred to as going "green" can help to significantly reduce costs, attract and retain workers, create new sources of revenue, and please shareholders and customers alike. From the smallest local outlet to the largest multinational corporation, companies realize that they must embrace the triple bottom line as a means of remaining competitive and profitable.

"I think sustainability has reached a tipping point where it has become much more of a principle and a recognized way of doing business," Broughton says. "It reminds me of where the notion of diversity was less than twenty years ago. During the 1980s, the concept of diversity was seen as new and not universally accepted. But enough momentum was built behind the business case that it ultimately became a principle. Today you never have to justify embracing diversity in the workplace. The same thing is happening with sustainability. What was once a fad has now become mainstream."

ADOPT SUSTAINABILITY BROADLY

While the idea of corporate sustainability is relatively recent, journalists, activists, and whistle-blowers have been encouraging change by shining a light on questionable corporate behavior for some time. Imagine what worker conditions might be like without the vocal efforts of people such as Upton Sinclair, Karen Silkwood, Cesar Chavez, and countless others like them. But the emphasis on sustainability as we know it today really didn't take hold until the late 1980s. That's when British author and consultant John Elkington, a leading figure in the sustainability movement, first coined the term *triple bottom line.* Since then we've seen corporations gradually switch from focusing solely on shareholders (those with a financial stake in the business) to also considering the needs of stakeholders (those directly or indirectly influenced by a company's actions).

Elkington's call for action wasn't answered overnight. For a long time operating in a sustainable manner was perceived as being too expensive, or viewed merely as a time-consuming public relations exercise that yielded little value. The tide is now turning—and fast. A recent report by KPMG in cooperation with the Economist Intelligence Unit found that 62 percent of companies surveyed have a strategy in place for corporate sustainability, up from just over half in 2008. Only 5 percent of corporations don't currently plan to create a strategy, while the rest are working on it. Interestingly, 44 percent of executives polled agree that sustainability is a source of innovation, while 39 percent see it as a source of new business opportunities. What's even more telling is that, contrary to popular opinion, about half of these companies insist that implementing sustainability strategies benefits the bottom line. Wayne Balta, vice president of corporate environmental affairs and product safety for International Business Machines, was even quoted as saying, "For every dollar we spend, we are getting $1.50–2.00 back."

Although it's difficult to pinpoint one single event that prompted a change in the corporate mind-set around sustainability, several factors have contributed:

- The longevity and long-term financial success of so-called social and environmentally conscious companies
- Increased regulation on environmental issues, corporate responsibility, and human rights practices
- Growing awareness of the importance of the triple bottom line
- Governmental and celebrity focus on taking care of the environment
- Fallout from high-profile corporate scandals
- Mounting evidence that sustainability efforts improve brand reputation and result in positive PR and word of mouth
- An increase in socially conscious investing and the tracking of these companies through such indexes as the Domini 400 Social Index and the Dow Jones Sustainability Index

The move toward sustainability is a global phenomenon that is even further ahead in Europe due to the ratification of the Kyoto Protocol in 2002, which perpetuated thinking about ways to help lower emissions. "You also see it in places like Brazil, which has relied heavily on alternative energy for years," says Broughton, who grew up in London. "And some of the largest manufacturers of electric vehicles are based in China."

CUSTOMERS FAVOR SUSTAINABLE BUSINESSES

So what does sustainability have to do with driving customer loyalty? A lot, as it turns out. Today's customers have a strong interest in doing business with companies committed to sustainability. The 2010 Cause Evolution Study by Cone found that when considering two brands of similar price and quality, 80 percent of consumers would be willing to switch to the more sustainable option. A national Capstrat–Public Policy Polling survey found that 59 percent of customers consider a product's environmental sustainability to be very important when making a buying decision, and 56 percent would be willing to pay more for a more environmentally friendly option.

"You'll find that increasingly customers will want to know what you're doing to enhance the triple bottom line," Broughton insists. In response, some of the world's biggest corporations now post annual reports on their websites showing what they are doing to make the world a better place. Starbucks, for instance, has long positioned itself as a socially responsible corporation. That message resonates with its customers who place a value on fair trade and environmental sustainability and are therefore willing to pay a slight premium for a cup of the company's java.

To meet customer demand, and demonstrate its commitment to bringing alternative technology to the rental car market, Enterprise has increased the number of electric and hybrid vehicles in its fleet. "Ensuring that the passenger vehicle remains acceptable and economically viable to society is a huge part of our drive toward sustainability," says CEO Andy Taylor. "We know that investing in new technologies now will create value for us, our customers, and the community in the future. In fact, more than half of our entire fleet consists of fuel-efficient vehicles." That includes thousands of hybrid vehicles and gas-powered cars generating at least 28 miles per gallon. Enterprise has also dipped its toe into car sharing with its Enterprise CarShare business. The service, found primarily on corporate and college campuses, provides hourly rentals, often using alternative-fuel vehicles. The company also has a ride-share vanpool program, where seven to fifteen coworkers can ride together, with each paying a low monthly rate. "The ride-share program helps to take cars off the road, reducing traffic congestion, commuter times, and driving costs," Andy Taylor says. "In many cases, the program works together with Enterprise CarShare, giving those who carpooled to work the option to rent a vehicle for an hour or two in order to run errands during the day."

Encouraging ride sharing and renting hybrids are two ways Enterprise is trying to get customers involved in the sustainability effort. Companies enlist customers to take part through numerous means, including recycling. Aveda, a beauty brand owned by Estée Lauder, has come up with a unique program in this regard that has been highly effective. The company sells its plant-based hair, skin care, and makeup products through a network of nearly seven thousand salons and spas worldwide. As a business founded on environmental principles, Aveda has long paid attention to its packaging. Its shampoo bottles and makeup cases use post-consumer recycled materials that can easily be recycled again. A few years ago, Aveda took its recycling initiative one step further. While a lot of consumer packaging can easily be recycled, most caps topping shampoo bottles, sodas, milk jugs, mayonnaise jars, and laundry detergents cannot. That's because they're made of rigid polypropylene, a plastic that the average recycling facility can't handle and must send to landfills. However, polypropylene *can* be recycled with the right equipment. So Aveda decided to start its own recycling program, collecting these caps at salons and other designated locations, melting them down, and then using them to make new caps and containers. Beyond helping the environment, Aveda's Recycle Caps program helps to offset manufacturing costs, making it an economically advantageous program.

EMPLOYEES VALUE RESPONSIBLE COMPANIES

Paying attention to the triple bottom line also drives employee loyalty and is an especially important consideration for younger workers. "Eighty percent of undergraduates coming into the workforce say that sustainability is one of the key performance indicators they consider about a company before making a decision to join the organization," Broughton notes. "By having a strong commitment to the triple bottom line, we are able to engage with these students. Today's grads have an attitude that they really want to influence the world for the better. Some feel they have to go work for a nonprofit in order to do this. We help them see that they can have a huge influence in the corporate world as well."

Numerous surveys show a strong correlation between engagement and environmentally responsible organizations. One reason is that employees of such companies partially view their jobs as contributing to a cause.

Starbucks, another early adopter of the triple bottom line, sends its employees out to work on various community service projects. It invites customers to join in the effort as well. Walmart, one of the first major corporations to make a significant commitment to sustainability, has found the campaign to be an important driver of employee engagement. Walmart launched a volunteer program for workers known as the Personal Sustainability Project in 2006. More than 1.3 million employees ultimately signed up to participate, making a commitment to recycle, eat more healthfully, exercise more, or even stop smoking. The program has evolved into what's now known as My Sustainability Plan and allows employees to automatically track and compare their efforts to other Walmart associates online.

Seven Steps to Implementing and Benefiting from Corporate Sustainability

- Use scenario planning to identify potential risks to your business—and new opportunities to exploit.
- Set ambitious targets and lead by example.
- Start measuring environmental inputs and productivity across your business.
- Tap into employee engagement, both internally and across business partners.
- Transform internal lessons into external products and services.

- Explore other benefits that can be derived from action on sustainability.
- Benchmark and report progress.

Source: KPMG Internal Cooperative

DOING GOOD IS PROFITABLE

As alluded to earlier, beyond earning the loyalty of customers and employees, operating in a sustainable way is actually more profitable. Bob Willard, a former IBM executive, consultant, and author of two books on the business case for sustainability, has attempted to quantify just how much additional profit can be generated by paying attention to the triple bottom line. In his view, the gains come from several areas—risk management, additional business opportunities, and cost savings generated by eco-efficiencies.

Willard calculates that large corporations with a focus on sustainability can realize a profitability improvement of at least 38 percent over five years. The opportunity is even greater for smaller and medium-sized companies—66 percent over five years. (These figures are a composite of profitability gains among companies that have adopted sustainability initiatives.)

Enterprise has certainly found its sustainability efforts to be financially beneficial. The company estimates it saved around $18 million from energy efficiencies in 2012 alone, up from $1.1 million the prior year. The goal is to get that number up to $50 million by 2015.

In order to help drive its sustainability efforts, Enterprise set up a Chairman's Task Force, comprised of department heads from fifteen cross-functional groups. The task force is responsible for developing best practices that can be implemented companywide to reduce both costs and the organization's impact on the environment. "Sustainability isn't a stand-alone department here," Broughton points out. "We try to get all of the relevant parties involved in the process. If you attempt to set up a sustainability department, it's less likely to be viewed as everyone's responsibility. The key to institutionalizing sustainability is integrating it into the existing infrastructure. Plus, you don't get noticed by the accounting team!"

Enterprise is committed to embracing sustainable practices primarily in three different areas: fleet, facilities, and technology. At the center of this is what the company has dubbed its 20/20 Vision, which calls for lowering overall energy use and related costs by 20 percent in 2015.

Specifically, Enterprise has set a goal to reduce its carbon footprint by 10 percent, cut natural gas and electricity consumption by 20 percent, and convert all airport shuttle buses to B20 biodiesel in this time period. In addition, the company has begun to look for ways to reduce its carbon inventory, plans to invest $150 million in sustainable construction, and is on a mission to plant fifty million trees in national forests throughout the United States, Canada, and Europe by 2056.

In order to monitor its progress on the conservation front, the company compiled energy use totals for all branches in 2010 and used this data to come up with an aggregate baseline. "We populate the information into a database we call BEN, for 'branch energy number,' which helps us to assess how much energy we use per square foot on a weather-normalized basis," Broughton says. "We have a portfolio of more than seven thousand buildings that use electricity, natural gas, and water. Our efforts are aimed at reducing our overall footprint." Enterprise has started with what it regards to be low-hanging fruit, such as installing energy-efficient lighting and trade dress. It has also moved the ECARS system over to energy-efficient thin client terminals, cutting its annual carbon dioxide emissions by 6.5 million pounds. Over time it will move on to bigger initiatives.

"We do a cost-benefit analysis for every potential upgrade and expect each one to pay off in five years or less," Broughton explains. "One complicating factor is that every facility is a bit different, so we have to look at every potential retrofitting project separately. Our branches are housed in very different buildings. Some are located at the bottom of multistory parking garages, and others are inside buildings where we're just renting a desk. Adding to the complexity is that we own some of our facilities, but a lot are on lease. At the end of the day, though, anything we do also has to make financial sense."

For newly constructed buildings, Enterprise adopted a set of guidelines that calls for using regionally produced materials with at least 10 percent recycled content, installing energy-efficient light fixtures, reusing old fixtures and furniture, installing water reclamation systems in automated car wash systems, and using organic compounds for paint, carpeting, and adhesives. Some of the company's newer buildings have been certified by the Leadership in Energy and Environmental Design (LEED) program, and all are built according to what's called the Enterprise Sustainable Construction Protocol, which sets out principles for building based on seven focus areas: materials, energy, sites, recycling, water, air quality, and process.

"We have long prided ourselves on our ability to run smart, efficient operations," says president and chief operating officer Pam Nicholson. "This sharper focus on sustainable management of our resources adds a great new dimension to the operational excellence that's always been so critical to our success."

Conservative and disciplined financial management is at the heart of Enterprise's approach to corporate sustainability. "Everything we do at this company is based on a long-term perspective," says Greg Stubblefield, the company's chief strategy officer. "We could make a much bigger song and dance by ignoring the return on investment and just spending money on efforts that grab headlines. But that would go against what sustainability means to us. The same value system of running other parts of our business applies to our sustainability strategy."

Many other high-profile companies have adopted similar goals targeted to making their business practices more sustainable in ways that also make financial sense. Nike has spearheaded efforts to recycle shoes, improve labor conditions overseas, and design its products using methods that generate the least amount of waste. Coca-Cola made a commitment to improve water efficiencies by 20 percent (a big deal considering that H_2O is the number one ingredient used in the company's beverages). Procter & Gamble has vowed to develop and market at least $50 billion in cumulative annual sales of "sustainable innovation products," which have an improved environmental profile. At last count, the company was just $10 billion shy of this goal. At the same time, it has reduced its overall energy usage, CO_2 emissions, waste disposal, and water usage by more than 50 percent.

BE SUSTAINABLE, OR FACE BIG PENALTIES

Demonstrating progress in the area of sustainability is important to retail customers, but it's also essential to business-to-business providers. "We supply some of the biggest companies in America, and we're asked all the time what we're doing to reduce our footprint and put out fewer emissions," Broughton says. "On top of that you have government agencies that require companies to mitigate issues relating to climate change. This has sped up momentum across the supply chain, where you're continually expected to help others reduce their footprint as well."

As climate change becomes an even more pressing concern, governments around the world are expected to adopt new laws around environmental issues. In the United States and elsewhere, lawmakers are weighing the benefits of carbon taxes or stringent greenhouse gas caps. In both of these scenarios, companies that do nothing to address their environmental footprint will pay a steep price that's sure to cut into revenues and market capitalization.

"Corporate America has started to reengineer its supply chain," notes Andy Taylor. "If you're a big company that's reliant on a lot of different industry categories to get your product out, you have the ability to influence those suppliers. Walmart, for example, has said that if you want to get a product on the store's shelves, you first have to demonstrate how you'll reduce your CO_2 waste."

To keep score on how companies are doing in this regard, several benchmarks have been created under such initiatives as the United Nations Global Compact, the Global Reporting Initiative, and the Carbon Disclosure Project. "We did an assessment of our top fifty customers, and about 48 percent have signed on to using the scorecard of one of these three organizations," Broughton notes.

Andy Taylor admits that continuing to improve Enterprise's sustainability score over time is a primary component of its long-term survival. "Our company's success depends on the availability of vehicles and fuel, and both must be acceptable to society," he offers. "That's why we are taking steps now to invest in the future, as part of our commitment to sustain our business and address those areas we touch from an environmental perspective." Taylor adds that the company's goal is to create "shared value," a concept that was popularized by Michael E. Porter and Mark R. Kramer and which is defined as "creating economic value in a way that also creates value for society by addressing its needs and challenges."

What are some ways you can help your company and customers save money by choosing and offering environmentally aware options? How might you gain a competitive advantage through your commitment to sustainability? What are some of the less environmentally friendly things you currently do that can easily be changed? And how can you improve your brand and reputation among customers and employees through your commitment to more environmentally friendly practices?

USE THESE LESSONS TO SHAPE YOUR SUSTAINABILITY PLATFORM

Noting that Enterprise has learned a lot about building a sustainable business through its efforts, Broughton encourages every business to consider following ten principles that have helped to shape the company's environmental platform:

1. Align your sustainability strategy with the overall mission of your business. Enterprise has always been focused on taking care of its customers and employees. Now it also is committed to taking care of those parts of the world touched by its business, diving into issues such as alternative fuels research and resource conservation.

2. Play to your strengths. Enterprise spends its time tackling issues directly connected to the automobile industry, where it can have the greatest impact.

3. Be fiscally smart. The company believes that it's not enough to just develop environmentally responsible vehicles and fuels. These solutions must be commercially viable. The same thing is true of energy-efficient building upgrades, which need to generate savings in a short period to justify the investment.

4. Understand and anticipate what customers want. It was demand from customers that caused the company to begin offering hybrid rental options and led to establishing a carbon offset program. (Enterprise, National, and Alamo customers can buy carbon offsets. The money is used to fund projects that in essence help to offset the cars' emissions, such as capturing and using methane gas produced by landfills to generate electricity or funding windmill projects.)

5. Never underestimate the power of employees. Enterprise keeps employees regularly updated on its sustainability efforts, and encourages them to inform the company about new environmental initiatives that might be of interest to customers.

6. Don't forget infrastructure. Before embracing clean alternatives, the company makes sure it has the infrastructure in place to support them.

7. Think long term. Enterprise views up-front costs as an investment in the future and doesn't expect them to pay off for five years.

8. Partnerships are important. Enterprise often partners with other organizations to provide new insights and validate its efforts. For instance, it has joined forces with TerraPass to administer the carbon offset program.

9. Localize your efforts. Enterprise realizes that what works in one market won't necessarily go over well in all of its branch offices around the world. Case in point: hourly car-sharing has a niche audience, working best to serve the needs of urban communities as well as government, corporate, and university customers.

10. Keep it simple. The company has found that some of the most effective environmental efforts are those basic, practical applications that lead to major benefits, such as switching to energy-efficient light fixtures.

FORM THE PILLARS OF YOUR SUSTAINABILITY STRATEGY

There are three pillars to Enterprise's sustainability effort: legacy, foresight, and innovation. *Legacy* represents the Taylor family's value system and the reputation it hopes to build on being environmentally responsible. To that end, the Taylors have pledged more than $120 million to important environmental causes over the past decade. *Foresight* refers to the company's decentralized way of doing business, its conservation program, and the investment it makes in the communities in which Enterprise, Alamo, and National operate. *Innovation* refers to the company's commitment to be as big and important in the rental car industry over the next half century as it was in its first. "Sustainability is going to be an important component of ensuring that we can be around for the next fifty years," Andy Taylor says.

While you hear about these efforts primarily from larger companies, Broughton insists the triple bottom line is something every business should be concerned about, regardless of size. But this commitment has to start at the top. "If your objective is to build a reputation for sustainability, that will lead you down one path," Broughton observes. "If you believe that operating in a sustainable manner is the right way to do business, that's a different idea. If your objective is cost savings, that's another component altogether. Some businesses hope for all three. Those that aren't reaching for any of the above probably don't understand the opportunity that is available to them."

Changes even the tiniest company can make include upgrading air-conditioning units, using more efficient lighting, changing out computer systems, using environmentally friendly supplies, and encouraging employees to recycle.

"This stuff isn't just for the elite blue-chip multinational companies," Broughton insists. "Trust me, I'm not a tree hugger or an environmentalist. This stuff doesn't come naturally to me. I believe in sustainability as a business strategy, and we at Enterprise have already seen the benefits."

KEYS TO DRIVING LOYALTY BY BUILDING A SUSTAINABLE BUSINESS

1. Focus on the triple bottom line—giving equal weight to your company's economic, environmental, and social performance.
2. Look to increase sustainability efforts as a way to reduce costs, attract and retain workers, create new sources of revenue, and please customers.
3. Find ways to promote your sustainability initiatives, so you can make the public aware of your commitment in this area.
4. Enlist customers to get involved through numerous means, including recycling drives.
5. Understand that employees of companies focused on the triple bottom line tend to be more engaged, since they view their jobs at least partially as contributing to a cause.
6. Perform a cost-benefit analysis on every potential effort that is designed to be more environmentally aware in order to make sure it will pay off in five years or less.
7. Be ready to demonstrate how your sustainability initiatives will also further the sustainability efforts of your customers.
8. At the very least, look for small changes you can make in your business, such as upgrading air-conditioning, using more efficient lighting, or changing out your computer systems.

Afterword

If one were to sum up the key traits that have enabled Enterprise to build on its legacy of success for nearly six decades, while maintaining a strong culture that drives loyalty by putting customers and employees first, it would largely come down to the following:

1. Be open to opportunity. Enterprise has always tried to think outside the box and find new ways to grow its business. However, during its first five decades, the company chose to grow organically, refusing to even consider taking on a major acquisition. When the chance to buy Alamo and National came up in 2007, Enterprise executives realized they had to be open to new ways of doing things in order to take advantage of changing market conditions and a once-in-a-lifetime opportunity to bring three unique brands with completely different target markets under its umbrella. The acquisition has proven to be phenomenally successful, largely because the integration of all three brands was done in a careful and calculated way so as to preserve the company's employee- and customer-first culture. This willingness to consider larger acquisitions has allowed Enterprise to continue to expand around the world. It has also put a renewed spring in the step of employees, who are excited that company executives are focused on keeping Enterprise a vital and growing organization.

2. Build a strong brand and stay in your swim lane. Over the course of five decades, Enterprise Rent-A-Car came to be known as the company that provided exceptional customer service by picking customers up and being there to provide a replacement vehicle when the customers' own cars were in the shop or otherwise unavailable. After the company acquired Alamo and National, it had to decide whether to keep all three brands or instead merge either or both into the Enterprise Rent-A-Car fold. At the end of the day, executives realized that all three brands catered to a distinct customer base that came to the rental experience with different expectations. For instance, National customers are generally business travelers who want quick transactions and prefer reliable technology to hand-holding. That's precisely the opposite of what Enterprise Rent-A-Car customers have grown accustomed to. As a result, Enterprise kept all three brands separate and further built out the respective unique business propositions of each, allowing the company to serve and cultivate a broader array of raving fans.

3. Empower employees, lead with empathy, and share success. Jack and Andy Taylor's approach to managing the workforce has always come down to this: treat everyone on the team exactly as you would want to be treated yourself. This means giving them the power to make decisions on the spot to resolve customer issues, while paying bonuses that allow even those at the lowest levels of management to benefit as the company prospers. But the company also believes in holding employees accountable for performance. In fact, bonuses and promotions are largely based on each individual's customer service scores, which is measured monthly through regular customer surveys. The company's empathetic management approach is built around listening, being open, and providing honest feedback about how one is doing on the job. Managers also provide regular communications so that everyone is on the same page in terms of the company's mission and culture.

4. Connect with your customers and employees through full-spectrum marketing. There are more marketing and communications channels at your disposal today than ever before. The trick is to use them effectively and in ways that drive additional customer and employee loyalty. Enterprise focuses on those marketing channels that resonate best with customers of each individual brand. For instance, since Alamo customers are always looking for good deals online, much of that brand's marketing efforts are dedicated to Web-related activities. By contrast, Enterprise Rent-A-Car has built the bulk of its business around more personal connections and partnerships with insurance companies and body shops, and therefore targets its marketing initiatives accordingly. Enterprise also uses its online communities to engage in two-way conversations with customers across all three brands, monitoring what people are saying online and working to resolve customer issues in real time. In addition, Enterprise offers special loyalty programs for each brand, allowing it to reward its most frequent customers and providing an effective means for marketing to an extremely targeted audience. Furthermore, Enterprise uses full-spectrum marketing to reach its large international employee base, developing an intranet site known as the Hub and its own internal television network.

5. Make decisions about growth and expansion by listening to your customers. To figure out where the hockey puck is headed in the car rental industry, Enterprise executives not only spend considerable time researching the competition but also are in constant contact with the company's customers, including its many corporate partners. It was from these conversations that Enterprise realized there was a strong demand by customers to do business with the company at more airport locations. Though Enterprise Rent-A-Car had a decent airport presence before the acquisition, buying Alamo and National allowed the company to nearly quadruple its number of airport locations overnight. When coming up with new services, Enterprise increasingly turns to its various social media sites to solicit instant customer reaction and suggestions. The company also ensures that any growth strategies stay true to each of its brands, and it makes certain not to overpay when considering any potential new acquisition.

6. Keep your eye on the triple bottom line. Though once considered to be a bit outside the mainstream, putting a major focus on operating in a sustainable manner has become an essential component of doing business today. Paying attention to the triple bottom line means giving equal weight to your company's economic, environmental, and social performance. While Enterprise has always tried to operate with an eye on sustainability, it put a major focus on this effort several years ago and has seen significant results. By identifying ways to reduce emissions, operating branches in a more energy-efficient way, and contributing to efforts that foster the notion of sustainability, the company has won the loyalty of those customers and employees concerned about the environment, while helping to lower overall operating costs and ensuring that its business remains viable for decades to come.

Acknowledgments

It's always amazing to think about how many people are involved in getting a new book into your hands. For *Driving Loyalty*, it all started with Christy Cavallini, Enterprise's vice president of communications. Christy immediately got my vision for this book and was a huge supporter from the start. Christy's boss, Pat Farrell, was equally instrumental in helping to bring this book to life. Pat and I worked together very closely on *Exceeding Customer Expectations*, and it is no wonder that Enterprise has since put him in charge of its entire marketing and communications effort. I also want to express my appreciation to Ira Robb, who initially introduced me to Enterprise and is an amazing entrepreneur in his own right.

Many Enterprise executives were very gracious with their time and expertise, including Ed Adams, Marie Artim, Lee Broughton, Laura Bryant, Rob Connors, Matt Darrah, Dan Gass, Rob Hibbard, Lee Kaplan, Craig Kennedy, John MacDonald, Steve McCarthy, Pam Nicholson, Mike Nolfo, Don Ross, Viji Samikannu, Jim Stoeppler, and Greg Stubblefield. In addition, I want to thank both Andy and Jack Taylor, and the entire Taylor family, for allowing me to tell the incredible Enterprise story not once but twice. I very much appreciate the trust and confidence you have placed in me to share with others the secret sauce you use to drive customer and employee loyalty.

On the publishing front, I again had the privilege of working with Roger Scholl, one of the best editors in the business. Thanks to the rest of the Random House team as well for their belief in this book and for helping to get the word out about it, including Tina Constable, Mauro DiPreta, Tara Gilbride, Paul Lamb, Michael Palgon, and Michael Nagin, who designed the great cover. At Literary Productions, kudos to Rossie Kay and Tom Perricone for your ongoing help, counsel, and support.

Finally, I want to thank you, the reader, for allowing me to take you on this journey to discover some of the techniques you can use to turn every customer and employee into a raving fan for your brand.

As always, I welcome your feedback and suggestions, both on this book and on other topics and companies you think I might be interested in writing about in the future. You can contact me by email at kirk@kirkkazanjian.com, through the book's website at www.drivingloyaltybook.com, or through my personal website at www.kirkkazanjian.com.

Index

About the Author

KIRK KAZANJIAN is an inspiring and authoritative voice on the latest trends in marketing, branding, and delivering excellent customer service in today's fast-changing and ultra-competitive world. He has written some two dozen books and is a top marketing executive for one of the world's largest financial services companies.

A lifelong entrepreneur, Kirk is a former award-winning television news anchor and business reporter, and has appeared as a guest on a variety of media outlets, including CNBC, CNN, Bloomberg, and other radio and television stations across the country. He and his books have also been featured in numerous publications, including *Barron's*, *Entrepreneur*, *Fortune*, and *USA Today*.

In addition to being a prolific writer, Kirk is a popular speaker and consultant on such topics as supercharging your marketing efforts, delivering excellent customer service, driving loyalty across your entire customer and employee base, increasing employee engagement, and making your company stand out from the crowd. For more information on Kirk, including details on how to book him to speak at your next event, just visit his website at www.kirkkazanjian.com.